The Well Traveled Guide

Wisdom, Tips, and Tales for Wandering the World

by Lynn Doerr

The author has made all efforts to present current and relevant information, but it is best to double-check processes and prices as things in the travel world constantly change. The intention of this book is to provide general direction on what to consider when traveling. For any health or medical questions, please consult with a physician or other healthcare professional. Any mention of individuals in the stories is based on the author's interpretation of the situation. No harm is intended with the sharing of these stories.
www.wanderlynn.com; wanderlynntravel@gmail.com

Copyright © 2024 by Lynn Doerr

All rights reserved. Printed in USA

No part of this book may be reproduced, distributed, or transmitted in any form or by any means, including any electronic or mechanical methods, or used in any manner without written permission of the copyright owner except for the use of quotations in a book review. Please purchase only authorized print or digital editions. The author appreciates your support of her rights.

First Dragonfish Publications paperback edition February 2024
First Dragonfish Publications digital edition February 2024

Book design by Greg Field
Cover Design by Domingo Morales
Cover photography and all photographs, except the author photo, by Lynn Doerr

ISBN 979-8-9897087-0-3 (paperback)
ISBN 979-8-9897087-1-0 (digital)

Published by Dragonfish Publications

Comments from Readers

"The style of the writing is personal and conversational; it's like you are listening to a friend. A lot of practical information is presented along with a good dose of humor and great story-telling. I found the many website links very helpful for trip planning. I think this book is a good fit for a mature age group who finally have more time to travel, but many may not be too experienced or may be traveling as newly single. However, any adult traveler would gain helpful tips... It was fun to read and made me excited for my next trip. I liked the positive vibe, which is so important in having a good travel experience." *Terry L.*

"Well written and really good information for a newer traveler or one that has primarily traveled in the first world. As a more seasoned traveler, I did find a couple of items that were either good reminders and/or helpful links." *Lauren O.*

"She's covered so many things to prepare for extended travel that the reader can rest assured there is nothing left undone. I really like the casual, light conversational tone throughout. Felt like a friend walking me through the how-to's." *Kari G.*

"It was engaging and had great energy that kept me reading. And the little details from the various adventures made it more compelling. Those details also give weight to her as an authority for traveling the world." *Elizabeth V.*

Comments from Readers

"The tone is perfect—conversational yet authoritative. I do feel like a friend is putting her arm around my shoulders and giving me her sage advice. For folks who are ready to move from planned travel to crafting their own adventures… giving them confidence that they can figure it out themselves and have a great experience. There is such a growing market for people who have always had their business trips planned or took family vacations and now are ready to go off on their own. But how do they decide where to go, what kind of things they can handle (is it a strenuous hike?), whether or not to get travel insurance … stuff like that." *Robin B.*

"It has great travel tips which are easy to understand and doesn't bog down in minutiae and still provides the needed info. And the short tales provided great practical examples of the 'why' behind the tips." *Susan Y.*

Dedication

For my Dad, who loved to pack up the car
and go, go, go . . .

The Well Traveled Guide

The Well Traveled Guide

Table of Contents

Chapter One: Introduction to Travel	8
Chapter Two: Deciding Where to Go	14
Chapter Three: Deciding How to Travel	22
Chapter Four: Passports and Other Relevant Documents	32
Chapter Five: Flights, Lodging, and Insurance	42
Chapter Six: Ground Transportation	58
Chapter Seven: Packing	68
Chapter Eight: How to Earn and Use Travel Points	86
Chapter Nine: Money	94
Chapter Ten: Health	104
Chapter Eleven: Technology	118
Chapter Twelve: Cultural Immersion	124
Chapter Thirteen: Extended Travel	132
Chapter Fourteen: Recommended Resources and References	152
Endnotes	167
Acknowledgments	170
About the Author	171

Chapter One

Young girl celebrating Diwali, Kathmandu, Nepal

The Well Traveled Guide

Introduction to Travel

The only people for me are the mad ones, the ones who are mad to live, mad to talk, mad to be saved, desirous of everything at the same time, the ones who never yawn or say a commonplace thing, but burn, burn, burn like fabulous yellow roman candles . . .
—Jack Kerouac, *On the Road*

I wrote this book for anyone—woman, man, or otherwise defined; single or in a relationship; young or older (old is a state of mind; older is a reality of living)—who wants to see the world but may not know where to start. Or maybe you've started to travel; your wings have carried you through the local forest, but now you want to fly higher and farther than before.

Maybe your intent in buying this book is to become a traveler. Not a tourist, but an individual whose purpose is to explore with curiosity rather than be a mere observer of the unusual and unfamiliar. You want to learn about and experience the world, not watch it. What would it be like to join the ranks of the intrepid such as Jacques Cousteau, Edmund Hillary, Amelia Earhart, Nellie Bly, and Ernest Shackleton? Well, let's not get carried away . . . but you must start somewhere.

How do you develop the heart of a traveler? I define the essence of a traveler (as opposed to a tourist) as a seeker instead of an observer. Maybe this describes you. Do you associate with a feeling the Germans call *fernweh*, a word to describe the longing for far-off places? Americans often refer to it as wanderlust, and it is a direct opposite to *heimweh*, another German word used to describe homesickness. Being of German descent, I may have been born with fernweh, so it seems fitting to describe the feeling I have when spending too much time

The Well Traveled Guide

in the same place, the itch that can only be scratched by boarding a plane and landing in a place with unfamiliar sights, sounds, smells, and sensations.

Travel doesn't have to be intimidating—it can be liberating, educating, and relaxing for many reasons. When you know how to prepare, venturing into the unfamiliar is a calculated adventure into fun, not a threat. Keep in mind this book is a guide to travel, not destinations (never underestimate the power of a good guidebook to give you country or city information and insights). I will share knowledge from the many years I've traveled and the many countries I've been to, offering both general and specific knowledge with a dose of reality from my own experiences. Just remember that your knowledge will grow as you continue to visit new destinations. I never assume I know all there is to know at any point in time. I constantly read travel blogs and newsletters, and I exchange tips with other seasoned travelers as we all continue to learn from each other.

I hope this book inspires you to seek new destinations, motivates you to collect passport stamps while immersing yourself in the curiosity of new lands, and advises you to travel smart and travel safe. There will be mishaps (I prefer to call them adventures), but being prepared for the minor upsets and being able to recover from the more-than-minor ones will grant you stories to share with others. And I hope you will pass on your knowledge and wisdom with the best intent. Best of all, you will discover the courage inside you and develop the confidence to confront the unknown, qualities that can serve you in all aspects of your life.

The Well Traveled Guide

TIP: Learn "Hello" and "Thank you" in the local language for every country you visit. When you throw out a *kamsamnida* in South Korea or *arigato gozaimasu* in Japan, you'd be surprised at how gracious people become since you've embraced their country by learning a few words of their language. And smile, smile, smile! Don't be afraid to laugh at yourself if you make a mistake.

Tale: Immersion into Travel

When I was twenty-six, I was lucky enough to have a job where I traveled every week. I was in heaven! Monday morning meant a new adventure, a new place to explore. Boarding that plane at the beginning of every week, I anticipated the rise into the air when I could settle back in my seat, staring at the erased white line on the horizon, before falling into a deep sleep until I awoke hundreds of miles away. I memorized flight schedules from city to city in the days when I had to call our company travel agent, Terry, every week to book flights for my upcoming assignments. Under the direction of my colleagues, I learned the strategies behind hotel and flight miles and how to negotiate the best deals to leverage into vacations, so I was able to take friends to Europe or the Caribbean islands, most of it for free.

But then, back in a time without smartphones and social media, the reality of working on the road started to have an effect on my ability to stay connected with friends at home. It was a bit of a drag when the only way to connect was a phone call and long distance was an extra charge. But still, I visited almost every major city in the United States and experienced New York City,

The Well Traveled Guide

San Francisco, Miami, New Orleans, and Seattle, all for the first time, along with a handful of cities I never intended to visit such as Fargo, Kalamazoo, Paducah, and Dothan. I found ways to keep myself entertained as I traveled, sometimes driving from place to place when the distance was short, seeing the United States from north to south and east to west. My afternoons were usually free since I had consulting meetings in the evening, and I would use the time to explore, visiting Graceland with its seven-foot blue velvet sofa, braving the mists of Niagara Falls on a cold winter day, exploring the San Juan islands via the local ferry to watch killer whales, and exploring numerous art galleries, museums, and zoos. I felt so lucky to have seen more of the U.S. than any of my friends had and had the bonus of frequent flyer miles that allowed me to extend my explorations into other countries, feeling more fearless to travel to Europe and beyond. How hard could it be? I had so many lessons yet to learn . . .

The Well Traveled Guide

Statue of Liberty, New York City, United States

Chapter Two

Male Lion, Etosha National Park, Namibia

The Well Traveled Guide

Deciding Where to Go

Life shrinks or expands in proportion to one's courage.
—Anaïs Nin

Many people already have a destination in mind—a dream or a plan, a place they've always wanted to visit. That can make planning easier. But it's always a good idea to do a little research before you spend the money, especially if you are traveling alone. If you want to find a location that is outside of the ordinary, subscribe to travel blogs and newsletters with destination reviews or read travel magazines, including *National Geographic*. I've stumbled upon exotic possibilities and expanded my desire to explore places before they've become saturated with tourists. To help others, I have created a newsletter where I profile areas I've traveled and share travel suggestions. You can sign up on the contact page of my website at www.wanderlynn.com.

You can also search multiple travel websites for ideas on specific activities to find your perfect trip. Or type in best places to travel for "Renaissance art" or "wine tastings" or "fly fishing," etc. There are travel destination lists for everything—scuba diving, biking, cooking, hiking, seeing art museums, you name it—including reviews of the many places you can have these experiences. There are so many possibilities to indulge your interests! In fact, as more and more people travel, there are trips designed for artists, cooks, and even dancers. The questions you should consider are:
- What do you like to do?
- How much activity are you seeking and how much can you tolerate?
- What would you like to learn?

The Well Traveled Guide

- How do you want to spend your day? (Some itineraries visit multiple sites in a short time and involve a lot of car/transport time.)
- What is the experience you are seeking?

Understand the best time of year to travel to your selected location. For instance, if you are traveling to Southeast Asia, it might be a good idea to miss the monsoon season. In a place like Cambodia, where it's almost always hot and humid, early January and February are cooler, but you may want to avoid the Chinese New Year as hotels can be booked far in advance. In Europe, find out what months are the biggest travel months for each country and plan accordingly. In Italy, everyone tends to flock to the beach in August. I try to plan for the shoulder seasons (spring or fall) when the weather is not too hot or cold and there are fewer tourists. But remember that traveling somewhere when the timing is not ideal will reveal another experience; although it may not be the one you were seeking, it might prove to be more exciting. Be open to the possibility of watching snow dust London streets in January.

Think about your tolerance for new things, including the food and not being able to speak the language. Start small and work your way up to the more adventurous places (a relative term according to your amount of travel). Or travel with a group to a place that sounds intimidating so you have guidance and company. Remember that people everywhere are pretty much the same in their needs. We are just trying to be happy in our lives—enjoying a good meal, taking comfort in a safe place to call home, and having people we can laugh with around us.

The Well Traveled Guide

Once you've picked a country, try to read about it before you travel—I suggest both nonfiction and fiction books to give you a sense of history and culture. You might find that customs that seem deplorable (what they eat, how they dress) are better understood when you realize the context behind the choices. It will also help you to identify with individuals you meet when traveling. The adage "walk a mile in another person's shoes" applies well when confronted with a new place.

TIP: Review flight and hotel options before deciding where to travel. I have found that some destinations only offer flights certain times of the year, or the number of connections won't work with my schedule. Be flexible. Also, think about staying just outside of a major city to save on your hotel, but research the available transportation options to reach more central destinations. For instance, I was staying in Sydney for New Year's Eve—a very popular and expensive choice—so I opted for a few nights in a suburban hotel located right on the commuter train line. It was a safe, quick, and easy commute in and out of Sydney, and I saved a few hundred dollars on my hotel.

TIP: Set a Google Alert specific to travel—for international or U.S. travel or whatever your travel interest is—and Google will send you email alerts with news links specific to your topic. It is a good way to stay posted on general travel advice that could be important to trip planning.

Tale: East Africa - Strangers in the Night

As a child, I was fascinated with animals. So, it's probably no coincidence that one of my earliest trips was a safari in East Africa. Kenya and Tanzania took the adventure of being around animals to a new level, backed with an element of danger.

It was late and it was dark. Very dark. I opened my eyes, and only the faintest of images began to form after a few minutes. Because of my snoring roommate, I also had in earplugs. Two senses robbed, and I was in a flimsy tent in the midst of the African Serengeti. But something had broken through the barriers and coaxed me awake. What was that noise?

Only a few hours earlier, our group had been enjoying our evening meal in our dining tent, laughing and discussing the great safari finds of the day. Our dessert was interrupted by the roars of lions somewhere in the inky black beyond the campsite. Lucas, our guide, looked very nervous.

"The lions are very close," he said.

Of course, we were all Americans, unfamiliar with the personal trauma of having someone you know attacked and eaten by a lion. The big cats were the favorites at the zoo, when safely contained in cages. We didn't fully appreciate how close and how dangerous they were. "RARRRRAAAGGHH!" The lions interrupted us again.

"We will be driving you back to your tents," Lucas announced. We looked at each other in surprise. The line of tents stretched seven long, and although they were a few hundred feet away from the dining tent, it was a short walk.

"Really?" I said. "Maybe we can just run to the tents." I liked to tease Lucas just a bit.

The Well Traveled Guide

He suddenly smiled as he realized I would not seriously run to my tent if he decided otherwise.

"Oh yes, you can run faster than the lion," he laughed as he joined in the joke.

Meanwhile, our other guide, escorted by a couple of our campsite staff, went to bring the Land Rover around for us. But we weren't quite ready to retire to our tents. We sat and talked and drank beers for another half hour. By this time, the roars had stopped. When we decided it was time to go back to our tents, Lucas felt it was okay to walk back. We all grabbed our flashlights and began moving as a group toward the tents. I was also searching the tall grass around our campsite, looking for tell-tale glowing eyes. There was only blackness. Linda and I entered our tent, the last one in the row, furthest from the fire, and took care to make sure both zippers were closed. A lion versus a zipper—that would be an interesting contest. We got ready for bed and were soon asleep.

A few hours later, I was wide awake and thinking of the lions. Despite the earplugs I could hear the distinct huffing, puffing, breathy sighs, and movement suggestive of a large animal. It seemed to be right outside the tent and, despite the possibility of some danger, I wanted to see it. But that would require venturing from the safety of the bed and walking oh-so-quietly to the back of the tent where a small flap covered the suggestion of a window. And then, perhaps, if I lifted it very carefully and strained my eyes to their limits, I might be able to understand what creature was in the darkness. I had to know what stood on the other side of the piece of fabric playing the part of the bedroom wall. I stepped as lightly as possible and approached the window. Would

The Well Traveled Guide

it hear me? I lifted the small flap slightly above eye level and rose on my toes to unveil the mystery. And there it stood, a giant Cape buffalo, about fifteen feet from our tent, only a thin curtain of fabric between us. And he was hungry. Settle down, I told myself, buffalo are vegetarians.

At this point, my roommate was also up and whispering to me, "What is it?" I tried to stare her down into silence, as if she could see the "hush" look on my face. I wasn't about to whisper anything, since I'm sure he could hear us moving around in our amateur attempts to be quiet. And I'm sure he could smell us. At the same time, he didn't seem to care that we were so close. He was hungry, and he continued to rip out chunks of grass, chewing and blowing softly. I could hear every stalk of grass being crushed between his teeth. I was tense, but it was excitement, not fear. Without the piece of canvas to separate us, I could have taken a few steps and laid my hand on his black back. But that was not an option, so I softly crept back to bed and appreciated the fact that he could enjoy dinner right outside our tent while we slept in the middle of the Serengeti, surrounded only by a piece of fabric. I soon returned to sleep and my roommate to her snoring. He had to hear that.

The Well Traveled Guide

Cape Buffalo, Kenya, Africa

The Well Traveled Guide

Chapter Three

Ancient city of Ephesus, Turkey

The Well Traveled Guide

Deciding How to Travel

Better to see something once than hear about it 1,000 times.
—Asian Proverb

We've already agreed that you are not seeking to become a mere tourist (not that there is anything wrong with relaxing and taking in the sights)—you seek to be a traveler craving a more complete experience. Starting global travel can be intimidating, and there are several approaches to travel, each appropriate for different situations. Traveling with a group may be the right introduction to bolder experiences, while traveling with friends or family might be the anchor you need to test the waters. Whatever you decide, there is no wrong way. With the right attitude, all travel is ultimately a positive experience.

Group Travel

Group travel is a great way to get your feet wet if you are new to travel, and companies continue to expand the types of travel offered. You can hike, scuba dive, horseback ride, bike, or kayak through a country (or enjoy some combination of multiple activities); you can paint, cook, or enjoy regional wines; and you can sit back and let someone drive you from place to place, stopping to view the most famous sights. Group travel is a good solution if you are traveling alone, have limited time, don't speak the language, or want to experience elements (such as home stays) that you may not have access to if traveling alone. One of the great advantages is meeting like-minded people who would never have entered your circle, becoming friends, and having someone to travel with on future trips. One caution: most companies suggest that they will pair you with a roommate for the trip to save you the single supplement

The Well Traveled Guide

(or as I like to call it, the "single punishment") fee. I've had good and bad luck. Despite earplugs that promise to block the noise of an intense rock concert, they don't always work to block out a stranger's snoring. On the other hand, it's a great way to turn a stranger into a new friend.

Suggested companies that I have traveled with in the past:
G Adventures (https://www.gadventures.com)
Offers a variety of trip types and extensive destinations, and and in some instances, you can book through a local travel agent.

Intrepid (https://www.intrepidtravel.com/us)
Tends to cater to younger travelers but they do include all ages.

Explore (https://www.exploreworldwide.com)
I've booked some great hiking trips through Explore and met people that I still travel with today!

REI (https://www.rei.com/adventures)
One of the best trips I ever booked was with REI. Their trips are active and tend to be more expensive, but if you have the money, I would splurge.

Exodus (https://www.exodustravels.com/us/)
Their clientele is usually English, and I have met some fun people on the trips. I've used them for hiking trips, and the guides are usually country-based and knowledgeable, making the experience one of being a personal guest. As of 2021, they include International Expeditions.

The Well Traveled Guide

Traveling with Friends/Family
Traveling with friends/family can work well if you have varying levels of travel experience, as you can learn from each other, but you need to make sure you can compromise, since it is not usually the democracy that you envision. One person may exert more influence on decisions, and you need to know that and be okay with it. Or one person may retreat from making any decisions, leaving all the planning up to you. The big benefit? It's great to have someone to laugh with and be a bit of support if things go wrong. Besides, when you're ninety, you want to be able to reminisce with someone about the time you went on a gallop through the forest in Romania or were lost at 2 a.m. in the streets of Amsterdam, missing curfew at your hostel.

Solo Travel
Solo travel requires a certain attitude of resiliency and resourcefulness. There are "gateway" trips you can plan to introduce yourself to traveling alone, such as a long weekend in a city close to home. It's not for everyone. I find that I am happy to be alone during the day as I can pick the specific things I want to do or see and can set off with a plan with no regard for the lack of company. The toughest time for me is dinner. After an exciting or interesting day poking through the ruins of a temple in Asia or hiking in the mountains of New Zealand, I crave company while enjoying a glass of wine over a delicious meal. I often feel that I am bursting with the delight of the day, and I want company to share in the joy of this good earth. This is the perfect opportunity to extend yourself—I have invited new travel friends to dinner, and no one has yet refused. It could be another man or woman traveling alone, or even a couple, but those dinners become a night of laughs and good cheer as we share little bits of our lives and other travel adventures.

The Well Traveled Guide

When you are alone you feel more vulnerable, but solo travel can be a cure for the isolation we often feel at home. Unfamiliar territory might drive you to act differently and expand your concept of what you do or don't do. I have ended up taking rides with people I have met on the plane or in the airport because I dared to start a conversation. Remember to be careful and trust your instincts—if something doesn't feel right, it's okay to bail. But most people in the world are good and are happy to help a lone traveler.

Extended Travel

Whether alone or with a friend, extended travel is for those with enough experience and/or guts to do the planning required to leave their home for a long period of time. And those who are willing to roll with the ups and downs of constant decision-making and the newness associated with going from place to place. You usually find your own routine and start to adapt it for each country or place you visit. This is what gives you a sense of control and security when every day is different and there are few to consult with if problems arise.

My routine? When I find a place to stay, I begin by unpacking certain essentials so they are convenient as I come and go every day. This makes any place "my" place and helps me to keep track of everything that goes in and out of my bags every day. If I stay somewhere a few days, I try to locate laundry facilities, and walk around to see where to buy water and breakfast. I make friends with the front desk staff and ask any immediate questions on the area. I have found the staff to be an excellent source of information, happy to share the best of their city or country. And, of course, there is the inevitable search for Wi-Fi. There was a time when I didn't rely on the internet for anything when I traveled.

The Well Traveled Guide

Like most things, there are positives and negatives with the internet: the positive of instant information, making it much easier to travel, especially when you're alone, and the negative of spending too much time looking at a screen rather than visiting an ancient temple or meeting other people to exchange information. As a traveler, you will find the right balance to keep your experience interesting without being isolating.

Travel Agents

Travel agents can be helpful if you are new to travel, have no idea where to go or what to do, or just want someone else to take care of the details. I have used travel agents to help with some bookings because they have a relationship with a property and can help make special arrangements. It's a win/win/win since I have less to do, the travel agent gets credit for the booking, and the property gets a customer they may have missed. And since most properties want the travel agents to send more guests (it's a business after all!), they are usually very accommodating to people making requests.

Volunteer Work

Another option is to do volunteer work in another country, sometimes referred to as "volun-tours." I began exploring this option as early as 2000, but it was a few years before I went on my first volunteer trip. I was on safari in Africa, and a woman in my group had started a volunteer organization conducting dental camps in Nepal. I told her I wanted to volunteer with her organization someday. The next year, I planned a hiking trip to Nepal, and I contacted her. Since her clinic was running while I was in Kathmandu, I stopped by for a visit and to see the clinic in action. It was amazing! Kids of all ages attended the well-organized clinic, opening their mouths for dental care. Despite witnessing the few inevitable tears from the children, I was sold. The

The Well Traveled Guide

following year, I booked a volunteer trip with her group in Nepal and then volunteered for three additional clinics in Vietnam, India, and Cambodia over the next several years. Global Dental Relief is the only organization that I've worked with—they are excellent, and the people I've met are wonderful.

My advice is find a group that requires you to do real work and includes work with the locals. Some trips seemed geared more to observing and may have a brief activity such as reading to children. I like to get my hands dirty, and I like Global Dental Relief because they are small enough to be personal yet big enough to make a footprint in the places where they hold clinics. I also know the money I pay to go on a trip is used for supplies and the basic necessities rather than a fancy office somewhere. Even though I am not a dentist, I enjoy working in the health care area and serving children for the long-term impact. We take dental health for granted, but most people in the world have very limited or no access to it, and something like a cavity can manifest into intense pain where the only solution is to pull the tooth. There is no question I'm helping improve someone's life when I work in a dental clinic.

Below are some suggestions for volunteer organizations:

Global Dental Relief (https://www.globaldentalrelief.org) They organize dental clinics for children in areas with little access to dental care. They include some sight-seeing days in their trips so you can experience the country you are visiting.

Go Abroad (https://www.goabroad.com) Many trips are geared to students, but you can sign up for their newsletter to see the options.

The Well Traveled Guide

Cross Cultural Solutions (https://www.volunteerforever.com/program/cross-cultural-solutions/) I first researched their trips in the late '90s, and they have evolved. They have many options for those interested in volunteer travel.

Together Women Rise (https://togetherwomenrise.org/learn/travel/) This organization holds local meetings where woman gather to learn about nonprofit efforts to benefit women and children in other countries. They also offer trips to specific destinations where members can see projects in action.

TIP: Start small and manageable—if you go too far outside your comfort zone at first, you might find the experience too challenging. If you know you're fussy, go for a more customized travel experience catering to higher-end clients. And if going alone, get your own room. Manage what you can but always remember to ask yourself, "Is this the worst that could happen?" The answer is "no," and instead of feeling angry or resentful, be grateful. I have watched people who have arrived rather stiff but soften over the course of a two-week trip as they see that even when the world is different, it is manageable and often full of unexpected delights and pleasant new friends with whom they can share experiences.

Tale: My First Group Trip

I had decided to go to Peru and hike to Machu Picchu. I can't even tell you why I picked Machu Picchu. Most people had never heard of the place. It was 1999, and the internet was still a new tool for many people. It was the first time I was using it to book an international trip, and I was going alone. I found a small company that booked trips to Machu Picchu, but I had so many questions, I had to call them several times to try to get a sense of what to expect:

"How strenuous is the hike?"
"Will there be a place to do laundry?"
"What kind of sleeping bag should I use?"
"How much luggage can I take on the hike and where do I store the rest?"
"What vaccinations or medication do I need?"

The list went on and on.

Even though I had traveled weekly for many years for business, this was an entirely new endeavor, and I had lots of questions. Although the people on the phone were helpful, they couldn't close all the gaps, and I continued to search for someone who could book my trip. I didn't speak Spanish, so I knew I needed some help with logistics. I was specific—I wanted to hike to Machu Picchu (many companies would only offer the train or even a helicopter to the village at the foot of the mountain) and go into the Amazon region. After all, I was in South America, why not do both?

I finally stumbled across a website for a company called Tread Lightly. I liked the name and what it suggested. I called the 800 number (remember when we worried about toll-free phone numbers?) and talked to a woman who was incredibly helpful. She could arrange the two parts of my trip as a solo traveler and could answer all my questions. I booked it.

When I arrived in Cusco, there was someone holding a sign with my name to drive me to my hotel. After the

The Well Traveled Guide

overnight flight, I was barely awake and happy to stumble into my room and take a quick nap before I began to explore the city. She had arranged a tour of Cusco and an evening meeting with the group I was to hike with for the next four days. Who knew that when I walked to the little office off the main square that I was to meet two other women who would still be my friends twenty years later? Even though I had started the journey as a single, I met a wonderful group of people for the four-day adventure. Although everyone from my hiking group left after the hike, and I went on to the Amazon region, we exchanged emails and kept in touch, leading to a couple more trips with one of the women and even eventually living in the same city as the other! You never know who you will meet when you dare to venture out alone.

And the hike? It was strenuous but certainly doable for anyone with a good level of fitness. Did we have trouble managing stairs for the next two days post hike, due to our aching quads and glutes? Yes—but every step was worth it. We spent hours walking on ancient trails through the mountains, each "trekker" geared to the hilt while our porters ran the same trail in front of us, carrying our camping bags and gear, wearing only flip flops made from old tires. And on the final day, when we summited the Sun Gate, staring down into the ruins of Machu Picchu, it wasn't just with a sense of accomplishment but a sense of awe from looking at this very old city, hidden in the mountains and valleys of the Andes where people had gathered and lived centuries before.

The Well Traveled Guide

Chapter Four

Tongariro Alpine Crossing, North Island, New Zealand

The Well Traveled Guide

Passports and Other Relevant Documents

Exploration is the physical expression of an intellectual passion, and it is the traveler's conceit that there is much wisdom to be gained in the investigation of this wide world.
—Unknown

Passports

Your passport is your gateway to leaving the country. And adventure! If you don't have one, what are you waiting for? It's surprising how many Americans don't have a passport. But not everyone is interested in exploring the world. Some people happily stay in the city where they were born for their entire lives. I sometimes wonder if this is why people can develop a sense of "us" versus "them" when it comes to people from other countries. One of the many positives of travel is the chance to meet and appreciate people from different cultures. It doesn't take many trips to learn that you have more in common with someone halfway around the world than you would think.

Now that you are curious to meet the Sherpas of Nepal or the African tribes of the Serengeti, it's time to secure a passport. It's easy to apply online at the Department of State website (https://travel.state.gov/content/travel/en/passports/apply-renew-passport/how-to-apply.html).

The U.S. Department of State provides the forms and information to apply for your first passport or to renew an existing or expired one. When scheduling a trip, give yourself enough time to apply and receive the passport. In the last few years, wait times have greatly increased because of the post-pandemic travel surge. The current recommendations, from the government website, are 10 to 13 weeks for routine service and seven to nine weeks

The Well Traveled Guide

for expedited service with an extra fee ($60 at this time). And this doesn't include mailing times. Also, if you already have a passport, be sure to check the expiration date, as many countries require at least six months of validity to enter the country. If your passport expires in June and you plan to travel in May, you will need to renew or obtain a new passport even if you plan to be home before it expires. I have met people who didn't take this seriously and arrived at the airport to be denied their flight. You don't want to be turned away from your flight or turned away from entering your destination country because of a passport expiration issue. Can you imagine the disappointment of a ruined or delayed trip, not to mention the extra expenses involved?

In case your passport goes missing while traveling, it's good to check in advance where the U.S. consulate is located in your destination city or country. Also, make a couple of copies of your passport—keep a hard copy in a separate bag and save a digital file where you could access it online to print a copy. It will make things much easier when it comes to replacing it.

If you're concerned about safety or potential travel issues for your destination, set a Google Alert for the country you plan to visit. Google will send an email with a link to any news items concerning your topic. You can look for additional information on the federal government's travel advisory site:
https://travel.state.gov/content/travel/en/traveladvisories/traveladvisories.html/

The Well Traveled Guide

TIP: If you expect to do a lot of travel, when applying for or renewing your passport, request the 52-page passport book. There is no additional cost, and it will save you the time and money of adding pages later or buying a new passport. It is possible to run out of pages—I've done it. Twice.

TIP: Some states in the U.S. will require a REAL ID or passport for any air travel within the country, so be sure to check your local requirements. For people in these states, a current driver's license does not meet federal requirements as valid identification for any government-related purpose. Different states mark REAL IDs in different ways, but it usually involves a star emblem. This site has more information: https://www.dhs.gov/real-id/real-id-faqs

TIP: Take a photo of your passport and save an electronic copy in a Google Drive or other accessible cloud-based storage. Or send yourself a copy in an email. This is a great backup if your passport goes missing.

TIP: When you go through customs or pay for a visa on arrival, always open the passport and make sure it is yours before you leave.

Global Entry and TSA PreCheck
If you live in the United States, you have probably heard of Global Entry and TSA PreCheck, but what is the difference? I can tell you that having Global Entry is like finding out you can drink a bottle of wine and have no hangover, like eating chocolate truffles and gaining no weight, like winning the lottery and paying no taxes . . . It's that good!

The Well Traveled Guide

Basically, TSA PreCheck can mean a shorter line through security. You don't have to remove your shoes, unload any computers, or pull out your little bag of shampoos and lotions to deposit in a special security bin. Global Entry is best for international travelers. You enjoy the TSA benefits for flights in the United States, but you go straight to a special kiosk on re-entry into the country for an expedited experience. While watching everyone else wait in line for passport review, you've already passed through immigration, used the restroom, made all your phone calls, and grabbed your bags (well, maybe), and are on your way. Magical.

The price difference between the two programs is only $15—it's $100 for the Global Entry program and $85 for TSA PreCheck, and each membership is good for five years (check prices because they may change).

To qualify for either program, you must go through a vetting process that includes a face-to-face interview with a U.S. Customs and Border Protection Agent at a designated center. There are more centers available for the TSA PreCheck process, and not every airport offers a Global Entry Enrollment Center.

The agent will ask you a series of questions, take your photo, and scan your fingerprints. Once approved, you will need to enter your number into the Known Traveler Number field when making airline reservations or on your profile page if you are a frequent flyer. This is necessary so that your boarding pass will reflect your status and let you use the expedited line. Not every airport has a TSA PreCheck line (incredible, right?), so review the list to see if your airport is included. As to Global Entry, in the post-Covid environment, appointments can be difficult to schedule, and some

The Well Traveled Guide

airports will let you meet with an agent when you return from abroad, whether it is for an initial interview or a renewal. Be prepared for a wait.

Check the options for the various Trusted Traveler programs here: https://www.dhs.gov/trusted-traveler-programs.

Visas

When you travel, remember that you are a guest when you enter another country. You are there because they have allowed you to enter, and they are under no obligation to do so. This is why you pass through customs and immigration and may have to purchase a visa when you enter (some are free).

There are a couple of options for finding visa requirements: Check the Department of State site (the same site you used to research applying for a passport), but also check the government site for the country you are visiting. Requirements change—a country that required a visa a few years ago may no longer require one. Or vice-versa. Again, who to let in to their country and how is the government's decision.

There are different types of visas—those you can apply for "on entry" and those you must apply for in advance. If you need to apply in advance, it usually involves sending your passport to the consulate or embassy or applying in person. There are also services, such as CIBT (https://cibtvisas.com) to do this on your behalf. You send CIBT your passport and the requested completed paperwork, and they handle the process for a fee. CIBT actually completes the process very quickly, reflected in the fee for the expedited service and speedy mail delivery. At least it's an option, and it is very helpful

The Well Traveled Guide

for last-minute or business travel.

Processes continue to change as countries add electronic options for tourists. And countries sometimes designate a visa type according to your purpose for the visit—business versus tourism versus study, research, or even missionary work. Different countries categorize and may even post additional requirements depending on what country you come from. Some countries, like China, have several distinct visa categories, so read thoroughly before selecting the correct one. If you are planning travel to a European Union country, starting in 2025, you will need a visa. This is a new process to enhance security and appears to be a straightforward online process with a small fee. https://travel-europe.europa.eu/etias_en

To allow for enough time to process a visa, learn the requirements when you begin planning your trip. Many countries also require you send a passport-type photo with the application. Keep in mind that most visas have an expiration date that you need to consider in your planning. If the visa is valid for 60 days, then you must enter and exit the country within that time period—it can be a tricky balance of timing. You don't want to risk having the visa expire by getting it too far in advance, and you don't want to lose your opportunity to travel to your chosen destination by waiting too long before applying. You also need to pay attention to how many days you can be in the country, as it can vary from country to country, and if you exceed the limit, they can impose penalties. Make sure you understand the requirements. If the country offers a visa on arrival, be prepared to stand in another line when you arrive and have the correct currency and fee amount (if applicable).

The Well Traveled Guide

You are on your way to receive your official stamp to enter the country!

TIP: I like to bring a couple of extra passport photos in case I need to apply for an extra visa while traveling or even to acquire special tourist passes for multi-day visits (such as at Angkor Wat). Digital photography has eliminated most of this need, but check the requirements in advance.

TIP: If you are traveling for several months, you may need to obtain your visa in another country because of the timing concerns mentioned. For instance, I was traveling for more than two months before I intended to enter Myanmar, which meant a visa I obtained in the U.S. would expire before I planned to enter Myanmar. Before I left, I checked for other countries where I could apply for my visa. Bangkok is close and a big city, and they had a consulate where I could get my visa. I planned to stop in Bangkok and allowed extra time for the process, which took two days—one day to drop off my passport and paperwork and a second day to return and pick up the visa. Be sure to check for any holidays when the visa office might be closed.

TIP: Some countries will not allow you entry if you have visited other countries prior to their country (certain Arab/Muslim countries and Israel; China and Tibet). Do your research, as this can change, and there are suggested ways to handle it. Sometimes it means visiting one country before another or having them give you a paper visa instead of stamping your passport.

The Well Traveled Guide

Tale: The Missing Passport

I always think certain things will never happen to me. Until they do. I was in Kathmandu with a group of volunteers. We had arrived to mentor a group of children at their boarding school during the Diwali holiday break. A few of us had gone out to explore, and one of the other women, Susan, wanted to stop and change some dollars into Nepalese rupees. We found a currency exchange, and Susan pulled out her dollars to make the transaction. The young man asked for her passport. This is normal protocol. She unzipped the outside pocket of her backpack, reached in, and came up empty-handed. She searched her entire bag but found nothing. I felt so bad for her but also wondered at the logic of carrying it in an outside pocket, easily reached by anyone walking by her. We went back to our guest house and informed the coordinators that her passport was missing—what a pain!

The next day we were back in the Thamel area, watching the ceremonies of Diwali and jostling through the crowds. I stopped to change some money and handed the young woman my money and passport. The woman looked at the passport, looked at me, looked at it again, and said, "This is not you." My face scrunched in disbelief. She handed me the passport, and I found myself staring into the eyes of an older blonde woman. Not me. It was Susan, who happened to be with me. "Well," I said, "I found your passport." It solved her problem, but mine had just begun. Where was my passport?

The visa process in Kathmandu consists of a long line with a few people behind a counter to collect money and stamp passports. I thought about how crowded and

The Well Traveled Guide

confusing it was when our flight came in, and we went to apply for our visas. As we waited in line, Susan had been in front of me. I must have mistakenly taken her passport from the counter when she walked off, while mine must have been given to the person behind me. I just assumed that the blue passport the visa people pushed at me was mine.

We called the airport to see if they had the missing passport. The good news was they did. When our local guide and I went there to pick it up, I followed him to the back offices of the airport, the behind-closed-doors area that most of us never see. We walked down a long hall to a small room where three men were seated around a table.

"We are here to retrieve the passport," my guide said. I stood there smiling while one man grabbed some keys to unlock a large metal cabinet. I saw him reach inside and grab one lonely passport sitting on a shelf. He opened it, looked at me, checked the photo, and handed it over. "How did this happen?" he asked. I laughed and said, "I have no idea." All three men started laughing as well. "But thank you so much for holding on to it," I said, while clutching it in relief. "Yes," the man said. "We knew you'd be back."

The Well Traveled Guide

Chapter Five

Stupas in Inthein, Inle Lake Region, Myanmar

The Well Traveled Guide

Flights, Lodging, and Insurance

To awaken alone in a strange town is one of the pleasantest sensations in the world.

—Freya Stark

Now that you've decided how to travel, it's time to leverage discounts or freebies to book an affordable trip. If you've decided to work with a travel agent or book a group trip, the prices are what they are, but you can still steer things to your budget and have an enjoyable trip. Consider staying a few extra days on either end of an organized trip so you have time to explore alone—it is the best sensation to walk the streets of a foreign city exploring the sights and watching the people. And if you can use points (covered in Chapter Eight - How to Earn and Use Travel Points), you can enjoy a few nights of free hotel or even a flight. Travel doesn't have to be expensive.

Flights and Airline Reservations

If you are booking your own airline ticket, many travel companies offer help and some discounts. But I advise you to start with airline ticket sites that allow you to review your travel options before you make final decisions. Be creative—explore the different combinations to reach your destination. For instance, if you are flying to Rome and the flight requires a connection, you could connect through London, Paris, Amsterdam, or Frankfurt. I've even booked separate one-way tickets to and from a destination to get the lowest fare. You could book a round-trip flight to Frankfurt and a separate round-trip flight from Frankfurt to Rome. I prefer direct nonstop flights, but timing and availability may present challenges. Depending on where you live, connecting flights may be the only option.

The Well Traveled Guide

TIP: Know the difference between a nonstop and direct flight. A nonstop is just that: it will not stop at another city on the way to your destination. A direct flight could have a stop in another city, increasing your travel time, especially if you must deplane for some reason.

Again, play around a little bit with the various pathways to your destination. I usually start with a flight search on Kayak, Google flights, or another such site. I'll make a few notes as to possible routings I may not have imagined. For example, when I flew to Dubrovnik, I looked at flights through London, Paris, Brussels, and Frankfurt. Flights through London can be more expensive because the taxes through Heathrow and Gatwick are higher. If flying to Asia, check your options flying east and west. Consider leaving from another airport within two hours of your home if that is an option. I'll also play with dates to see if there might be nonstop flights at certain times of the year when demand is higher. For example, some airlines will have nonstop flights to sunny islands only in the winter.

TIP: Before booking flights on airlines that are unfamiliar, check the airline safety ratings at this site: https://www.airlineratings.com. If you work for a global company, check with your company's travel department, as they usually have requirements on which airlines are allowed for business travel. If the company deems the airline to be unsafe, I would avoid that airline.

If you are using frequent flyer miles, you need to think about interesting options. (Check Chapter Eight–How to Earn and Use Travel Points.) The set itineraries that the airline site offers may not be the best. I usually choose to sort results by "shortest travel time" because long layovers can be brutal. Be sure to pay attention to the taxes on your ticket. This is the only fee on the "free" ticket and can range from $30 to $200. Again, Heathrow's taxes can be a few hundred dollars versus less than a hundred through another airport. You just need to balance your priorities; it might be worth a little extra in taxes to have a shorter layover. There are also airport hotels such as Yotel, where you can rent a room to sleep and shower on a long layover. If you are lucky enough to fly business class (with or without points), there are usually showers available in the lounge room to make your layover more tolerable. Another option is to purchase a day pass to gain entry into a lounge.

TIP: If the best flight option includes a long layover, check the feasibility of leaving the airport for a day tour. Many cities in Europe make this easy by providing luggage lockers in the airport or train station and by providing easy access to the city by train or shuttles. Some even have day trips designed for layovers! Check the arrival airport website for more information.

There are a few airports that require visitors to pay taxes when leaving the country. Check this site: https://www.tripzilla.com/countries-departure-tax/77780, as you may need to keep some local currency to pay for your departure taxes. They usually only accept cash in the country's currency. You don't want to make the mistake of changing all your money into your own currency and then having to change it back just to pay the tax. More and more airports/airlines are including taxes in the ticket price, which makes it easier on travelers.

Suggested sites to check for flights (many will let you set alerts):

Kayak: https://www.kayak.com

The Well Traveled Guide

Expedia: https://www.expedia.com
Momondo: https://www.momondo.com.au
Google Flights: https://www.google.com/travel/flights
Going: https://www.going.com
Skyscanner: https://www.skyscanner.com

TIP: Know your rights as a traveler. For instance, in the EU, there is a regulation, (EC) No 261/2004 (https://eur-lex.europa.eu/legal-content/EN/TXT/HTML/?uri=CELEX%3A32004R0261), stating when you can receive compensation for a flight canceled by the airline. Most people don't know these rules and never apply for compensation. Look at Articles 6, 7, and 8. There is some guidance from the U.S. Department of Transportation (https://www.transportation.gov/), but it's not as encouraging. It's usually up to the airlines. I have found that a well-documented letter explaining the situation can result in compensation if the fault is that of the airline. Weather doesn't count, but maintenance issues are covered.

Lodging

Hotels are so . . . yesterday? But are they? Although there are so many options for an overnight stay now: Airbnb, Couchsurfing, hostels, homestays, etc., hotels are still a mainstay for lodging. The number of apps and websites available can make this aspect of travel seem overwhelming and confusing. Ratings make it easier for you to assess a place to stay, but you need to pay attention to the dates and consider who has posted the review. Sites such as Trip Advisor post such a mix of experiences, things that are a small nuisance to one person can be a huge obstacle to another. I try to be very fair and balanced when I post reviews, and I encourage all users to do the same. For example, "Tiny shower but the bathroom was spotless" is fairer than "The shower

The Well Traveled Guide

was so tiny that I could barely fit. This place is awful!" Welcome to older hotels in Europe!

I have used Airbnb in a few instances and had good luck finding a safe and clean room with a good host, but many times have found the options to be expensive compared to a hotel for a single traveler. I know many families and couples have had good luck with accommodations when they need a place for multiple people. As with anything, there are scams, and it is important to carefully check your options and the fees (such as a cleaning fee) before you book. For those traveling on a budget, I've had good luck with hostels. Again, check your options as you may share a room with multiple travelers, which can include members of the same sex or a mix of men and women. And be sure you have somewhere to lock any valuables or keep them with you at all times.

If you have points, that probably means you have access to a worldwide chain hotel. (Check Chapter 8–How to Earn and Use Travel Points.) One good thing about booking with a chain is that there are few surprises. You understand the level of service offered, and it's easy to book a room and know what to expect when you arrive. If you're picky about certain things, then look for hotels that match your requirements. Go to the website and ask questions. Another perk of chain hotels is that they may be more willing to store luggage for an extended time. I was able to leave a bag for a month at a hotel in Bangkok while I traveled in Myanmar because I was a member of their rewards program.

I've booked many small hotels in Europe by going directly to the hotel's website and emailing my questions.

The Well Traveled Guide

Remember that most hosts want you to be happy, and they will do their best within reason to accommodate. I've had small hotels warn me about small rooms (the kind where you can wash your hands while sitting on the toilet; convenient but somewhat self-defeating) and steep narrow stairs for an upper floor room. If I know and I make the choice, then I'm fine because I know what to expect. I don't have the budget for the Emirates Palace hotel in Abu Dhabi (although I did have a gold-dusted cappuccino there) or any of the top luxury hotels in the world, but I'm constantly delighted by staying at small hotels with an excellent staff that make me feel very welcome.

Things to think about when looking for a place to stay:
- Safety – Is the hotel in a busy central area rather than on the fringes or down a dark alley? Busy areas are usually safer, especially if you are traveling alone and expect to be going out for dinner or coming in late. Sometimes it's hard to tell from a map, but reviews will generally yield some information on whether people felt safe there.
- Distance from airport and main sights – If you are not driving, how will you get from place to place? I like a hotel that allows me to walk to main sights, good restaurants, and public transportation. Distance from the airport may or may not be an issue, depending on transport options. I've stayed at places two hours from the airport and booked transfers to make things easier when I arrive, but I arranged hotels close to the airport (with a shuttle) for the night before I leave. A two-hour drive at 3 a.m. is not the best option if you have an early flight home, but I have done it.
- Cancellation policies – I prefer a hotel that will

let me cancel up until a few days in advance. I don't generally expect to cancel, but if there is a flight or travel delay or cancellation, I don't want to incur a charge.
- Photos of the venue – This is a bit of a deal-breaker these days. There is no reason a hotel should not offer a photo of the room you are booking.
- Cleanliness ratings – When I see several complaints about cleanliness in the reviews, I move on. Enough said.
- Price – How does the price compare to that of other similar hotels in the area? Remember that the "stars" rating for hotels refers to amenities, not necessarily how nice or clean it is inside. For instance, hotels that offer breakfast, soaps, and other niceties will have more stars. But a basic hotel that is neat and clean may be all you need for your stay. Being flexible about amenities will give you more options for better prices.
- Breakfast – It is very common in other countries for hotels to offer breakfast, and it is becoming more common in the U.S. Although I realize that they do compensate for the cost in the room rate, I love being able to go downstairs and have breakfast in the morning rather than having to go out on the street and forage for food. What can I say? I'm not a morning person and prefer a simple breakfast, so the less hassle, the easier for me. And when I'm traveling alone, it is not usually a social event.
- Amenities – Wi-Fi is a must have these days. I saw one evaluation that said something to the effect that Wi-Fi is expected; a TV is not. Do you want toiletries in the room? ((I'll address this in Chapter Seven on Packing - you should be using refillable

The Well Traveled Guide

containers you brought from home rather than generating trash.) More and more hotels have refrigerators in the room, which are handy for cooling your water or other drinks and for keeping some fruit or breakfast yogurt. Some hotels offer laundry services, but some have washers and dryers (even better and cheaper), a nice treat when traveling long term. Star ratings are based on amenities, so the more offered, the higher the star rating, and this has little to do with the other criteria you might be evaluating. Parking may be another consideration—free or a fee? Everything adds up.

- Overall reviews – Read the reviews from a couple of different booking sites as well as Trip Advisor to get a good sense of what you will find, keeping in mind the perspective of the reviewer. And leave reviews for more obscure places, remembering to be fair and describe the good and the bad. If you had a bad experience but the staff corrected it, be sure to mention this. Problems will inevitably arise, but addressing and correcting the issue is important.

Suggested Hotel Booking Sites:
https://www.booking.com
https://www.agoda.com
https://www.airbnb.com

TIP: Be nice to the check-in staff! Tell them about your trip or adventure and tap into their knowledge, especially when staying in the smaller places. I stayed at a hotel in Darwin, Australia, and after a lengthy chat with the desk agent (who turned out to be the manager), he upgraded me to a suite! I had a room with an upstairs and a downstairs all to myself. Completely unnecessary,

The Well Traveled Guide

but much enjoyed after three days of extreme heat and humidity in the wilds of Kakadu.

TIP: Discover the "transit airport hotel." If you anticipate a long layover or an overnight stay in the airport, I highly recommend a transit hotel for a nap (or overnight) and a shower. They are usually cheap, and it gives you some downtime from the cacophony of the airport when doing extended travel. Yotel is one example. You can usually find accommodations by googling the airport by name and searching for transit hotels. I used the Yotel in London when I had a long layover between overnight flights, and I've used the transit option in the Singapore airport when I had a late-night arrival flight from Bali and had a 12-hour layover before my morning flight back to the U.S.

Travel Insurance

When it comes to travel insurance, just say "yes." Even if you have health insurance that will cover you overseas, you will want to have emergency evacuation insurance. What does that mean? If you are hiking or traveling in a remote area and you need to be evacuated because of an injury (this stuff does happen—a friend's daughter had to be helicoptered to a hospital after a rock-climbing fall where she broke her foot), it will be covered. The last thing you want to negotiate in an emergency is how to pay for medical services. This type of insurance is not too expensive, and many organized trips require it and provide the insurance company, although you usually have a choice to find your own within the parameters they dictate. World Nomads is one company I've used in the past. Another suggestion is to check with Insubuy (https://www.insubuy.com.) They offer different packages depending on your needs.

The Well Traveled Guide

Also check your insurance options through your credit cards. Many will cover aspects related to your airline ticket and travel-related emergencies such as flight delays or lost luggage, but no health emergencies. It's good to review the details in depth and look for situations that might be relevant to you. The COVID-19 situation created a lot of angst with global travel, since pandemics are not usually covered as a reason for cancellation—not that we've had one in almost 100 years! Fortunately, many companies worked with customers, and many anticipate that it will affect future travel in new ways. Read the fine print on any policies before signing.

Tale: Les Misérables, the American Tourist Version

"Je ne sais pas," I repeated for at least the third time. What was I saying? I was trying to say, "I don't know," and even threw in some "Je ne comprendre pas," to further emphasize my confusion. The uniformed woman with the furrowed brow was speaking in a sharp and loud tone. My friend, Nida, kept repeating, "What is she saying?"

I finally managed to understand something about a "billet," and I held up my ticket. That didn't seem to be enough, as she was pointing at Nida, saying, "Donnez moi votre billet." Meanwhile, crowds continued flowing around us, barely paying attention as everyone hurried on to their destinations. We, however, were denied. Finally, a short slender woman hurrying by paused, as she must have overheard our conversation. She stopped and asked if we needed help. And she was speaking English!

"Yes! YES!" I said. "You speak English! My French is not very good, and she seems to want a ticket, but I can't understand the rest."

The Well Traveled Guide

It is a bit unnerving to have some official harassing you in another language, but at least she wasn't carrying a gun. The helpful young woman began conversing with the uniformed woman. "Ah, yes, she wants your friend's ticket for the Metro."

Nida's voice was dialed to at least eleven, maybe twelve. "I threw it away! We just came through the turnstile! And, . . . I was being responsible. Throwing my trash away!"

"Are you sure you threw it away? Check your pockets. Or did you stick it in your bag? I still have mine. We just walked through!" I was hoping that she had been too preoccupied to throw it away as we talked about the evening we had been planning for a couple of days. The helpful young woman remained calm as she said, "If your friend can't find her ticket, you will have to pay a fine." Then she lowered her voice, "They always look for tourists because some of them jump the turnstiles . . . or like you, they don't know they have to hold their ticket until the end of the journey."

"Well, I'm not paying the fine! I bought a ticket!" Nida said as she frantically began checking her pockets. I wasn't sure what to do and hoped that Nida would be able to produce the precious bit of paper. I looked around on the ground to see if she had dropped it. There were no ticket stubs laying around us. Suddenly I remembered to ask the helpful woman, "How much is the fine?"

"Four hundred francs."

Mon dieu! That was about $70! We didn't have that much money with us—we had just paid for dinner, and this was before the days of convenient ATMs. "Nida, we

The Well Traveled Guide

have to find that ticket. I don't know if we have enough money with us to pay the fine." The transit cop continued to glare at us. Who was this feminine embodiment of Javert? Images of French jail danced through my head. Would bread and water translate into croissants and Perrier? The French know how to do everything with style. Even this transit cop had on a smart little scarf.

"And we're going to be late." I turned to the woman to explain, "We were trying to get to the theatre—we have tickets to Les Misérables."

The helpful woman turned to the policewoman, pleading on our behalf. The policewoman with her tight lips just kept shaking her head. As far as I knew, shaking meant "no" in the French culture also. Our translator turned back to us.

"I've tried to explain, but I think she means for you to pay the fine or you will have to go to the police station." I felt bad holding this helpful woman hostage in such a desperate situation. "Thank you so much for your help. We've wasted enough of your time. We will try to find the ticket, and if not, we may have enough cash to pay the fine. I just hope they will let us buy our theatre tickets with our credit card." They were holding our tickets at the theater. It had been an arduous phone conversation to secure the tickets, and now it seemed they would disappear less than an hour before the show.

"It was no problem. Good luck!" she said.

Yes, "bonne chance" to us. I could see she was worried as she hurried away. But, after all, there were better amusements in Paris.

The Well Traveled Guide

What had started as a pleasant evening was becoming sour very fast. Nida had meant for the show to be a treat for me—a thank you for taking her on this trip. We had been friends since college, and I thought it would be fun to go to Europe with her, so I offered to use my thousands of frequent flier miles to secure a free round-trip ticket for each of us. She had seen Les Mis twice in the U.S.; she loved it and thought it would be so perfect to see it in Paris. If only we could make it to the theatre.

There was one last place the ticket could be—the trash can. "There—I think that's where I threw it. I'm finding that stupid ticket!" Nida went over to one specific can and started to rummage through it. Fortunately, it was not a full can, and there were limited bits of cast-off food in it. Nida was grabbing at ticket stubs, showing them to the transit cop and saying, "Here! Here!" The cop continued shaking her head. "Non, non," to every paper offer. Nida and I looked at each other, and my stomach was in knots. How could the ticket not be there? I thought for sure the officer must be lying. Nida continued to dig, offering stub after stub, each one refused. By now, Nida was furious. She was shouting "HERE! HERE!", offering every bit of crumpled and discarded paper. And still she was denied. She finally took the entire plastic bag from the sturdy metal can and dumped it on the subway floor. The uniformed woman silently watched as Nida picked through the trash, organizing it into two piles—possibilities and refusals. Even though the situation looked desperate, I started to help. Now the woman had two people shoving stubs in her face, and she shook her head at each one. Nida's face was red, and she was shaking. Every bit of paper had been reviewed and still nothing. It didn't seem possible. In a final gesture, Nida scooped up the entire heap of trash, shoved it in the bag and plunked it

The Well Traveled Guide

back in the can. "This is ridiculous! I came all the way to France to jump a turnstile and steal a fifty-cent train ride?" She reached into her purse and pulled out her wallet, her hands still shaking with anger. "How much is the fine?" she spat at the woman.

"That lady said it was four hundred francs. I'll pay half," I said. I don't think I had ever seen her so mad. And rightly so. We both felt that we were the victims of some tourist scam. But what could we do? French jail was not the way we wanted to spend the evening. I was so thankful that I had managed to hold on to my ticket, or we'd be paying two fines.

She shoved her francs at the ticket cop. The woman took the money and was on her way. Nida and I raced down to the platform to catch the train to the theatre. We were both too shell-shocked to talk until we settled into our seats. I tried to think how to refer to what had happened. "Well, we've had our little adventure. By the time we get home, I'm sure there will be police dogs and handcuffs and a night in jail." I looked sideways at Nida, and she turned slightly to look at me. And then we started to laugh. By the time the show was over, I acknowledged that Javert was rather likeable compared to the transit cop.

When we returned to our room later that evening, I grabbed my guidebook to see if it mentioned Metro cops. And there was the warning we had failed to notice.

"Hey Nida, listen to this. 'Be sure to keep your ticket until the end of the journey; you'll be fined on the spot if you can't produce one.'" Every adventure has a lesson. Read the guidebook thoroughly.

The Well Traveled Guide

Moulin Rouge, Paris, France

The Well Traveled Guide

Chapter Six

Ox Cart, Myanmar

The Well Traveled Guide

Ground Transportation

Tourists don't know where they've been, travelers don't know where they're going.

—Paul Theroux

Buses, Trains, and . . . Horse Carts?

Whether you are seeking transportation options from the airport to a city, or just within a city, explore the benefits of using local trains and buses when feasible. In many places, the options are clean, quick, and affordable. For instance, if you plan to go to Seoul or Tokyo, there are excellent bus services from the airport to many hotels in the city. The buses are very clean and modern and considerably cheaper than taking a taxi. You can find ground transportation options by checking the airport's website, a city travel and/or tourism site, or the information desk in the arrivals sections of the airport. If you decide to rent a car, more information is below.

Buses

One of the biggest obstacles with buses is making sure you understand the ticketing system. The basics you will need—some sort of pass, card, ticket, or exact change; you will need to know where to purchase this ticket (such as at a tobacco shop in Rome); where to find the bus you need; and how to know when you've arrived at your stop.

I usually carry a map with me when on a bus so I can watch the streets and will know when to ring the bell for my stop. If you've mastered the bus system in any major city in the U.S. or other western country, it's pretty much the same. I do remember being confused about the system for trolleys in Germany. Luckily, we figured it out because once we were on the trolley, we saw a transit officer checking to make sure people had tickets. If you

The Well Traveled Guide

have a guidebook, check the information. Or just google "buses in New York" (or wherever) to find more information. One of the fanciest bus rides I encountered was a drive from Chiang Mai to Chiang Rai in Thailand. Although it was only a couple of hours, my ticket price included a donut and a drink served by a bus attendant!

Trains and Subway Systems

The great advantage of speaking English is that many transport systems in other countries will have signs and information in their own language and in English. It makes it possible to take subways in places like Beijing where the native characters would be hard to translate. Almost no one speaks English in China, so you can't rely on asking strangers for directions, but the subway is easy to use. Overall, most underground systems are fast and efficient, and I prefer to use them whenever possible. Although most ticket kiosks are easy to use once you understand the logic, the first encounter might be . . . confusing. While doing business in Tokyo, my colleague and I decided to take the subway to the office one morning. We found the station, found the kiosks, but we couldn't buy our tickets because we were confused by the machine! We had to walk back to the hotel and ask the concierge. He revealed a key step we had missed. Once we walked back and bought our tickets, we were on our way. I always think these things will be intuitive, and they usually are, but there is no shame in asking for help.

And while it's easy to take the subway, some countries present more challenges when taking a train from city to city. Having taken trains throughout China with a small group—an interesting and very affordable experience—I decided it would be much faster to fly. Spending twenty-four hours on a Chinese train loses its charm

The Well Traveled Guide

when the intercom system bleats a loud wake-up call at 8 a.m., and you realize the disgusting smell is stale smoke infiltrating the car from people sneaking cigarettes in the space between train cars. No one is supposed to smoke on the trains, but since every man in China seems to smoke, I guess they feel it is useless to enforce it.

European trains are another story. You can buy tickets online or at the station to travel from city to city. The trains are modern, clean, and fast. And there is *no* smoking! Most train systems will have a website accessible in English, although sometimes the tickets are a little more expensive. When traveling in France, I used my modest command of the language to book cheaper tickets on the French site and used Google Translate to decipher some of the more technical language. I saved a little money and felt the victorious gratification of having overcome a traveling obstacle. Check out The Man in Seat Sixty-One website (https://www.seat61.com/index.html) for all questions related to train travel—this man is truly the train guru! His site gives information and tips on train travel, since not all websites are as user-friendly when translated to English. For instance, for women traveling alone on some overnight trains, you can book a ladies-only compartment. And online ticketing does beat the days when I had to send off for a Eurail pass by regular mail.

Horse Carts, Motorbikes, Tuk-Tuks, and Ferries

As you work your way to less developed countries, you will find more options in carriage. The horse cart is popular in places like Egypt and Jordan. I look for a healthy horse and a driver who treats his horse as a business partner, not a tool. In Asia, you can climb on the back of a motorcycle taxi, and although the driver may be sporting a helmet, he usually does not extend

The Well Traveled Guide

one to the passenger. The proper protocol is to hold the bars on the back of the seat, rather than clutch the driver in a death grip as he zooms in and out of traffic. Yet another option is a tuk-tuk, which may exist as a small cart pulled by a motorcycle or a man on a bike. Some of them can feel quite precarious as the driver dodges traffic, throwing you from side to side in the back. I try to assess the risk potential before agreeing to hire any of the above. Safety is still a luxury in many places, and road injuries are a major concern in developing countries. If it looks too dodgy, there is usually another option. Safety first!

Ferries are commonly used to cross rivers or larger bodies of water, for example, to take you from island to island in Greece, not a bad way to spend an afternoon. It also provides another opportunity to meet fellow travelers and trade stories and travel tips. Ferries can take more time, but there is always the benefit of seeing dolphins or other sea creatures. Just be sure to check the schedule in advance to make sure it fits with your travel needs.

Hiring a Driver

Another option is to hire a local driver. Some countries will not allow a tourist to rent a car. When I was traveling in Myanmar with a couple of friends, we hired a driver to take us between a few cities. It was cheaper and more comfortable than some of the other options, and we could make stops along the way. I found the drivers to be safe and courteous, and, although the vehicles were a little older, it was a good option for us. The other benefit is that you have someone with you who speaks the local language and knows where to stop for gas, food, and restrooms. We were able to find drivers by checking with our hotel. I have friends who have

The Well Traveled Guide

done the same in India or in other Southeast Asia countries or in Africa.

Renting a Car

Well, you've decided to embrace your adventurous streak! Driving a car in another country is not as difficult as you might think. It helps to have a co-pilot, since even with GPS, signs and directions can be confusing, but it can be managed alone. The goal is to find a company that has safe cars and transparent rental policies. There are multiple low-cost options available from an internet search, but they may be in locations that are difficult to access or may have more restrictions on where you can pick up or drop off the car. I also make sure to check that they offer GPS in English (many do). You can also opt to use your phone if you have service in that country, but make sure you can plug into the car for charging, as it may require an adapter.

As to the rules of the road, it is a good idea to do a little research beforehand to understand the driving culture. I tend to avoid car rentals outside the U.S., but I have rented cars in a few countries and managed to get through the weeks unscathed. I consider myself to be a good driver—aware and safe, which makes it easier to adjust in another country. (No texting and driving!) I rented a car in New Zealand, where I had to drive in the left lane and on the right-hand side of the car. My brain adjusted quickly, and once I had left the rush of Auckland, I was fine. I also drove in Italy, and many friends were aghast, thinking that all Italians drive like Mario Andretti. That wasn't the case. I found it to be more like the U.S. in that people tend to drive faster on the roads they know. If I was going the speed limit in a hilly section of Tuscany and someone wanted to pass me, they waited until it was safe, and they made their

The Well Traveled Guide

move. There was no vehicular stalking as sometimes happens in the U.S. My biggest worry was parking tickets, since I couldn't read the signs!

Keep in mind that most cars overseas have manual transmissions. If you don't know how to drive a stick (a lost art in the U.S.), then make sure you find a car with automatic transmission. It will probably cost more, but tackling new roads in a new language is probably enough of a challenge without also learning to drive manual as well. Also, check the trunk space, since many cars are smaller and can only hold smaller bags. I had a small Fiat in Italy and became a bit of a logistical goddess in figuring out the exact configuration for my bags in the trunk. I didn't have much luggage, but the trunk was very tiny.

Before you leave your home country, check to see if you will need an international driver's license. I did not need one for the countries I was in, but some car rental companies may require it. You should also check with your own car insurance company to see what coverage they offer and determine which credit cards offer supplemental insurance covering international car rentals. Some credit card companies will require you to turn down any supplemental insurance at the car rental counter for their insurance to be active. If you've purchased travel insurance, check their policy on car rentals in other countries. I purchased travel insurance that included car rentals in specific countries. As an extra precaution, take photos of the car before you drive off in case there is a question about any dents or dings upon return.

The Well Traveled Guide

Tale: Driving in Italy? Prego!

When driving in Italy, there are many opportunities for misunderstandings. However, it is a bit unfortunate that on my last trip to Italy I was driving alone and there was no one there to laugh with me. Or, more accurately, at me. In a country where I could manage about six words in the native language, I still decided to rent a car and drive myself to a small home in Tuscany where the friend of a friend had agreed to lend me his house for a few days.

There were obstacles—finding a company in Florence close to the train station where I could pick up a rental on a Saturday, locating the correct rental car company while dragging my bags across the Italian sidewalk obstacle course, mastering the logistical constraints of an itsy bitsy Fiat trunk, and relying on GPS to guide me to a rather basic address located in the hills outside of Florence.

Before I even left Florence, I was shamed into asking the car rental attendant for assistance as any address I offered the TomTom GPS was unacceptable. The attendant was able to type the precise combination of numbers and the street name to get me on my way. And he was kind enough not to laugh outright at me for not being able to do the same. Who knew it would take several hours to reach a destination only thirty minutes away?

Although the car claimed to be an automatic, it had an option to drive as a manual. I found it was easier to drive as a stick shift for handling the hills outside Florence where the energy of my little Fiat did not seem to quite match the demands of the hills. Fortunately, the

The Well Traveled Guide

little car seemed to handle it fine as long as I didn't try to rush. As I wound my way through the little clumps of houses and shops, my GPS claimed I was fast approaching my target. And then the message we all celebrate, "Your destination is on your right." I turned to see a field bisected by a long driveway with no house in sight. This didn't seem to match the description in the email my host had sent me.

After stopping the few people I could find to ask for directions, including a trio of ladies walking along the rather deserted road, some men in a van, and another stop at a small chapel, the mystery of my intended destination remained. Should I continue to wander for hours? The homeowner had provided me with the neighbor's phone number, just in case I had any problems finding the place. After almost an hour and a half of wandering, I had to admit defeat and make the call. But first, I had to find a cell signal. I drove to the top of another hill and called the number. When Andreas arrived to guide me to the destination home, I realized I had been only a couple of miles away, yet I never would have found the place on my own. And Andreas confirmed, "The GPS is not good for this address." Expectations realigned.

That was not the end of my driving adventure in Italy. I had to tackle Siena and the restricted areas where cars were not allowed with the handicap of not being able to read any signs posted in Italian. A definite conundrum! And there was the matter of identifying unleaded gasoline when filling the tank. Thank goodness for full service stations. And on my final day in Florence, as I navigated my way back to the car rental garage, I had a policeman blow his whistle and start to shout at me in Italian as I crept onto another street unaware that I

The Well Traveled Guide

was not allowed. I rolled down my window, flashed a big smile, and said, "I'm sorry, I don't speak Italian." I was instantly graced with his own Italian smile as he pointed and said in his lovely accent, "This way! This way!" pointing me to an escape. Within minutes, I was gliding into the garage greeted by a warm "Buongiorno!" from the parking attendant who had originally helped me. He seemed a bit surprised that I was smiling and wasn't wrapped in bandages from a week of mishaps. Finally, it was time to turn in the car. I felt like I had just won the Olympics rather than only conquering the wilds of Tuscany and Florence in a small Fiat. A rather thankful "Arrivederci" and a flawless resolution to my adventure.

In retrospect, it was, in a word . . . hilarious. New day, new obstacles, prego! Without adversity, travel is just another day on the road. I'll admit that I'm always seeking a little adventure, and it's only when things go astray that a trip becomes an adventure. At my hotel in Chianti, the hotel clerk spent time giving me some focused directions and suggestions on what to do in the area. I laughed while telling him about some of my misadventures earlier in the week, and he smiled at me and said, "These things make us stronger people." So right. It was empowering to find my way alone, and it was empowering to ask for help. How else would I have met the warm embracing Italians that make it so easy to travel there? Driving is driving, but there are still the cultural and geographical adjustments that take time. And in the end, there is the consolation of gelato when confronted with frustrating obstacles. Would I drive in Italy again? Yes! But I'm hoping to recruit a navigator next time.

The Well Traveled Guide

Chapter Seven

Young boy dressed for Buddha birthday celebration, Leh, India

The Well Traveled Guide

Packing

One's destination is never a place, but a new way of seeing things.
—Henry Miller

I have a confession: I am a notorious pre-packer. I'm not sure if there is a support group for people like me, but I will happily live with my addiction. Since I have a guest room, about two weeks before I leave, I begin throwing everything on the bed that I think I'll need for my trip. That gives me time to see if I need to buy anything and sort through how much I'll really need—as in, do I need to bring two blue T-shirts? I make sure that I have everything coordinated, and then I start subtracting. If you subscribe to any travel blogs or newsletters, there are endless recommendations on how to pack. In this chapter I've summarized a general approach to packing to help you think about the obvious and offered some practical recommendations that can be helpful depending on the type of trip.

TIP: To make sure you account for everything, start with your feet and work your way up your body to mentally check what you will need. What shoes, socks, slacks/shorts, tops, underwear, etc. should you pack? Don't forget your head—including sunglasses and a hat. For toiletries, go through your daily routine and then add items, such as a first aid kit, to prepare for special circumstances.

How to Dress for Cultural and Weather Considerations

Before you even pack your bags, do some research on what is most appropriate for the culture as well as the weather. In Southeast Asia, even though it is very hot and humid, it's not culturally appropriate for women to

The Well Traveled Guide

wear shorts. In fact, you will usually only see young boys in shorts. Women wear long pants or dresses (over the knee or longer); men wear long pants. This is also important when visiting cultural sites, since many require you to cover your knees or ankles, and even shoulders and arms. In Bangkok, some sites, such as the Royal Palace, rent long skirts to women as they do in Rome when visiting Saint Peter's Basilica. And in the Middle East, the Muslim countries are more conservative when it comes to women's clothing. A long-sleeve or three-quarter-length sleeve shirt will be more appropriate than sleeveless or short sleeves. You can invite unwelcome stares and even looks of disgust if you show too much skin. Some attitudes toward tourist attire are relaxing as more and more people travel, but I try to be respectful.

There are lots of recommendations on how to pack, and I read through them periodically for new ideas as I constantly refine my own list. What is the common strategy? Less is easier to carry and less expensive to transport. If you desperately need something, you can buy it. And it's fun to leave room for a few country-specific additions, which might include a sarong (for men and women) when visiting temples in Indonesia.

So, how do I pack less when I need to plan for every situation? You always hear that you need to "layer." Think about it—if you have a short sleeve T-shirt, with a long sleeve T-shirt over it, then add a fleece, and a rain jacket, maybe a scarf, you'll be in good shape for weather around the 40s Fahrenheit (~5–9°Celsius) if you are walking around. If you are planning for lots of outdoor time in inclement weather, you may need to add a heavier jacket, but I have found the above combination works well and is very adaptable.

The Well Traveled Guide

Again, be conscious of cultural norms for the country, which are usually more restrictive for women than men and might mean no tank tops even in hotter climates. It's easy enough to bring a lightweight long-sleeve shirt to wear over a tank when necessary. As more and more clothing manufacturers offer quick-dry fabrics and wicking material, it's even easier to pack light and use the sink to wash out clothes on the go, meaning you carry less weight.

I would recommend leaving jeans at home unless traveling to a cooler climate. Jeans are heavy, may mark you as from the U.S., and cannot easily be washed in the sink to dry overnight. The same "I'm from the U.S.!" assumption might be said for running shoes/sport shoes, but I have noticed more sport shoe attire in other countries over the last several years. It's important for your feet to be comfortable, so if running shoes work for you, bring them along.

The thing to remember is to pack basics that can apply in most situations. Don't bring lots of things for "just in case." For women, I suggest bringing one dress or skirt to have something dressy (over the knee will work in most countries). There are so many good options at outdoor stores (such as REI or EMS in the U.S.) that you don't have to feel too frumpy in travel clothing. Men only need a pair of khakis (not cargo pants) to serve as something dressy. Having at least one "smart" outfit gives you the flexibility to take part in more cultural activities. I keep one nicer shirt with a sweater and a skirt for when I plan a nice dinner somewhere and don't want to feel like I've just hiked in from the hills. Even if I have. A quick shower, some mascara, lipstick, a scarf, and a skirt, and you feel like a smart local. You might even be able to fool them!

The Well Traveled Guide

Luggage

Let's talk about luggage. Your considerations should include size, durability, ability to lock, ease of transport, and flexibility. In general, I try to check one bag and bring a small backpack on the plane. Again, you will see many philosophies on how to pack, whether or not to check a bag, and whether to use a backpack versus wheels. I've probably tried every combination depending on the type of travel. They all work—you just need to figure out what is best for you and your trip. Not everyone is suited to carry a backpack, but it is a great way to be flexible.

TIP: Find bags that you can lock. Some backpacks don't have zippers that will allow you to lock them, or they have separate compartments that don't allow for locking. Check this, as it's always nice to have the option and keep wandering hands away from your goods.

Before you leave, check the airlines you will be using for their carry-on and checked bag policies. These policies are inconsistent from country to country and airline to airline. In the U.S., you are usually allowed 40 lbs (about 18 kg) for a carry-on bag, while other countries only allow about 15 lbs (7 kg). In fact, if you are flying on some carriers from the U.S. to an international destination and have a connecting flight, this policy will apply, and you may have to weigh your bags in the connecting city and pay a fee if your carry-on is overweight. This happened to me when flying from Philadelphia to Fiji. I had to connect and change to a partner carrier in San Francisco and had to recheck my bags. Fiji Airlines required me to weigh my carry-on, which was packed full. And overweight. Because I had stashed an extra bag in the outside pocket of my

The Well Traveled Guide

carry-on, I was able to remove enough weight from the carry-on to meet the weight requirement. The irony was that I was still carrying on the same amount of weight—it was just divided between two bags. Don't try to make sense of some of the rules. It will make you crazy.

Luggage Rules:
- Flexibility is important. It might make sense to have two medium-size bags versus one large bag.
- I always bring a smaller bag that can be used on the return trip as a carry-on for any goodies I buy while traveling.
- ONLY TAKE WHAT YOU CAN CARRY BY YOURSELF. Bags with handles (even on back packs) are flexible enough to carry or grab if needed. (The one exception I encountered was when boarding a boat in Myanmar that required walking across a skinny little board from the dock to the boat with my luggage. I let the nice young man who worked on the boat carry it for me. He was used to walking that skinny little board while carrying bags or other heavy items.)
- Use compression bags, Ziploc, or compartment bags (packing cubes) to keep items separate and to make more room. They can also keep your items dry when your bag sits on the tarmac in a rainstorm. I've used compression bags for years and like the way they help me save space and organize my clothing.
- DO NOT PUT VALUABLES IN CHECKED BAGS. This includes medications, money, equipment such as computers, electronics, and jewelry. Also, many airlines do not allow certain batteries in checked bags. Always check airline requirements before traveling so you can accommodate. There can be some unusual

The Well Traveled Guide

requirements based on the airline.

For a five-month journey, I had a wheeled carry-on (for my camera equipment, medication, change of clothes, extra shoes and boots, and 3 oz toiletries), a very slim backpack (for my computer, Kindle, and a few necessities on the plane), and a medium-size backpack that I could slip inside a duffel bag for my checked bag. The duffel bag had just enough room in one end that I could add items from the wheeled carry-on to the checked bag to meet the weight requirements for my wheeled carry-on overseas.

I usually also have a small bag in my backpack for cords and other electronics-related gadgets. A plastic bag or Ziploc also works well. Don't feel like you must buy a separate bag for everything. Look around the house, and you might be surprised at the hidden treasures you have that work well for packing. For instance, I found that small bags given to me with a purchase of a purse or shoes make excellent packing bags for shoes. And then I'm never mixing dirty shoes with the rest of my luggage.

TIP: I have found myself in the situation where I needed to store a bag for a few hours or even a few weeks. In the case of a few hours, many airports, bus stations, or train stations still have lockers where you can store a bag. If you need to store your bag/s for longer than a few hours, I've left a bag in hotel storage for several days or several weeks after staying at least one night as a guest. I then return to retrieve my bags as a guest for a final night. Example: When I was traveling from Thailand to Myanmar, I had two bags but only wanted to take one since I didn't need everything in both bags.

The Well Traveled Guide

I stuffed one bag with the things I didn't need and left it at the hotel in the bag storage for an entire month. My strategy was to find a hotel that would allow this, stay there for a night or two before I left, then return for a final night or two at the same hotel. Although there were some services in Bangkok that would allow bag storage, it was cheaper to stay at a more "expensive" hotel and have the service for free. In my case, I found an international chain hotel where I was already a member of their guest program. Of course, I locked the bag, but the reality was there wasn't anything in the bag I couldn't stand to lose.

Laundry
Don't worry! There are plenty of options for doing laundry, which is why you only need to take about three to five days of clothes with you. At a minimum, you can wash out your clothes in the bathroom sink, but don't forget a plug for the sink as they don't always exist (or work) at your lodging. You can try to use a sock to plug the drain, but it's not the best solution. Some hotels offer some sort of laundry service, whether it's a washer and dryer on site (rare), an expensive service where they charge per piece (I never use this service), or in many Southeast Asian countries, the hotel will send your bag to a local who charges by the kilo. This is my favorite solution! I found a small hotel in Thailand where I would hand over a bag of laundry in the morning (basically all but the clothes on my back) and retrieve it when I returned in the evening, at a cost of about $2.00. And of course, there are laundromats where you can do laundry yourself, a more typical option in places like Europe. Pack clothing that doesn't need ironing, is easy to roll, and is made of wrinkle-resistant fabric.

The Well Traveled Guide

What to Pack
I usually break my items into three groups:
- Clothing
- Toiletries
- Gear (a rather nebulous yet essential group)

For clothing, I base my packing on these scenarios:
- Sightseeing and casual daily attire
- Activities such as hiking, biking, or water-based sports
- Nice dinner or cultural event requiring something beyond backpacker basic
- Volunteer work (probably optional on most trips, but do check to find out what type of clothing might be best. There could be cultural preferences based on interactions with the local people and, depending on the type of work, you may want to have a separate set of clothes.)

Clothing
This list has served me for a few weeks to several months:
- Shoes: Shoes are always the most challenging and the most important, especially if you're active like me. Baseline: Sturdy walking shoes, some type of sandal/flip-flop suitable for walking in hot climates (if you will be active, you may want something with straps so you don't lose a shoe), one pair of sandals/flats that can dress up an outfit for dinner, and some slippers/flip-flops for the bath/hotel. Optional: hiking boots.
- Two slacks: A pair of black travel pants which I use as "dress" pants if necessary (just make sure they aren't cargo pants); a pair of khaki/tan travel pants.

The Well Traveled Guide

- Two capri pants: Black (again, make sure they are plain enough to be dressed up) and another pair of khaki/tan or other neutral color.
- One pair shorts: A pair of walking shorts made of travel material will be very versatile, since short shorts are not well accepted in many countries. The travel material means you can wash them out and they will dry overnight.
- Skirt or dress for women/Nicer slacks for men: This is for the times you want to eat somewhere a little more upscale or attend a cultural event. For me, this happens enough that I'm happy to have this extra outfit.
- Shirts: Three-quarter-length sleeve tops are very versatile. I usually bring a couple of those, one to two long sleeve tops/sweaters, and about four short sleeve tops. Maybe one tank top that can also be layered. Mix solids with patterns. The great thing about a patterned top is that it hides dirt and stains. If you're committing to only a few shirts for several months, this can be important. I also try to bring shirts that aren't too fitted since they will work well in more conservative cultures. This is where you can add some color!
- Socks and underwear: Three to four pairs of socks (two extra pair of hiking socks if appropriate); five pairs underwear (so you don't have to do laundry every night); two to three bras (one sports bra if you are active).
- Pajamas/T-shirt and shorts for sleeping
- Fleece jacket
- Rain jacket (rain pants if hiking)
- Swimsuit
- Optional: Thermals for colder climates which double as pajamas; scarf (may be more fun to buy one along the way); hat and gloves

The Well Traveled Guide

- If you have hanging clothes, put them in a long plastic bag (such as a dry cleaner bag), which helps to keep them clean and wrinkle free.

Toiletries

A word about travel sizes. Regulations for carry-on allow for 3.4 oz (100 ml). A container of shampoo that size will last about two weeks (I have shoulder length hair). I pack all "leak-potential" containers in Ziploc bags so if something opens, nothing is ruined. In fact, you can use the quart bag required for carry-on toiletries. As to containers, I prefer those with a twist-off cap, since the flip-top caps can sometimes open and ooze contents.

- Sunscreen
- Toothpaste/toothbrush/floss—The little travel tubes of toothpaste that are 0.8 oz (23g) will last about two weeks
- Deodorant
- Body lotion
- Face creams/moisturizer—Small bottles will last a long time!
- Razor—You can protect the blade with a binder clip
- Shave cream
- Shampoo and conditioner
- Body powder
- Soap for hotels that do not provide. I also collect a few small bars along the way that I stick in a plastic bag. Or you can wrap them in a plastic shower cap from your hotel.
- Lip balm
- Brush/comb—I use a small folding brush
- Insect repellant—You may need a mixture with DEET for some countries (30 percent should be adequate)
- Makeup and a small mirror

The Well Traveled Guide

- Tweezers, nail file, manicure scissors
- Small sewing kit
- Safety pins
- Small bottle of detergent/Woolite (something such as Dr. Bronner's has multiple uses) or Tide Pods (in a small sturdy container for laundromats); you can also use shampoo in a pinch; Tide Stick to remove stains
- Travel towel—Always good to have a backup for beaches, etc.
- Q-tips, cotton balls
- Hand sanitizer (preferable to wipes, which generate extra trash)
- Kleenex, toilet paper—In many countries, public restrooms do not have paper. I usually take about half a roll, press it flat, and carry in a baggy in my backpack.
- First aid kit—Moleskin (for blisters), Band-Aids, Neosporin, cortisone, ace bandage
- Medications—acetaminophen, aspirin, ibuprofen, Pepto Bismol, Imodium, etc. Consult with a travel clinic for additional meds such as malaria pills and an antibiotic appropriate for the region you are visiting.

TIP: If you are not sure how much shampoo, etc. to take, do a test run before your trip. Fill the container with your normal shampoo at home and keep track of how many days it will last you. Then you know exactly how long it will last and how much to take. I was surprised to find that my little travel bottle of shampoo lasted 17 days—and that only applies if you need to wash your hair every day. Bottom line, there is no need to take an entire bottle of shampoo, conditioner, or lotion. Many hotels provide these items, and even if you

The Well Traveled Guide

must use hotel shampoo for a couple of days, it will not destroy your hair. In general, avoid using the hotel provided products as it produces more plastic trash, unless you know that they recycle the containers.

Gear
- Ear Plugs—Always remember and never forget. You can thank me later.
- Mask/snorkel—Optional; I have my own so I like to take them if I know I will be snorkeling or diving.
- Camera, instruction book (or bookmark online), cables, charger, batteries, photo cards, etc.
- Cell phone, ear buds, charger, SIM cards (from recent trips to add time)
- Computer/notebook and case, charger, flash drives/external drive
- Kindle and charger
- Plug adapter
- Glasses
- Journal/notepad and pen
- Plastic envelopes for receipts/tickets/documents
- Headlamp/batteries
- External charger
- Water bottle/Collapsible water bottle (very handy and easy to pack)
- Luggage locks/bag tags (even small ones for your backpack). If you are U.S. based, you'll need a TSA approved lock for your checked bags unless you are willing to sacrifice a lock if they feel the need to inspect your bag. I've lost at least two locks in London because the TSA lock doesn't apply there. So, carry an extra one in case security in another country cuts your lock. For backpacks and bags I'm not checking, I'll use any combination

The Well Traveled Guide

lock. Be sure to keep track of your combination, it's easier than keeping track of a key.
- Guidebook—Paperback or load to Kindle
- Small Swiss Army knife and spoon (if not included)— Remember this must be in a checked bag!
- Duct tape—You can wrap it around a pencil to have a good amount that won't take up too much space. Duct tape is an amazing "fix it" tool.
- Hydration tablets—If hiking or for dehydration associated with intestinal distress
- Portable laundry line
- Money belt
- Extra duffel/bag for carry-on souvenirs
- Trekking poles—If hiking
- Sleeping bag liner—Provides extra warmth and a safe cocoon for questionable bed linens
- Zip lock bags—Multiple uses and reuses
- Sunglasses with UV protection
- Sink stopper/plug for doing laundry in the sink
- Small travel umbrella—Can also be used for the sun

For the Plane

- Passport—Make a copy to pack in a separate bag; also, email a scanned version to yourself or store in a Cloud drive such as Google for additional backup if lost or stolen
- Visas for the country you are visiting, if needed
- Credit cards/ATM cards
- Vaccination card (if applicable)
- Driver's license for car rentals
- Plane tickets or boarding passes (if not electronic)
- Cash
- Travel insurance documents
- Neck pillow

The Well Traveled Guide

- Change of clothes if you are checking a bag (just in case a bag goes missing)
- Snacks/gum
- Reading material/books—My preference is to take my Kindle. If you prefer a book, check used bookstores or thrift shops for cheap books. There are many almost new books, and you will find current novels and nonfiction books for a few dollars. You can leave the books at hotels for others to read once you've finished.

Tale: What Not to Pack

We had finally managed to coordinate schedules and flights, and we were on our way to Europe. Europe! It was the backpacking trip I had fantasized about for years, the trip my friends from wealthier families were gifted for college graduation. Or just because. Of course, at that point in my life and my friend's, as working professionals, our backpacking trip was only about two weeks long because our jobs only allowed that tiny amount of vacation. Sigh.

My friend, Nida, arrived at O'Hare from Atlanta a day before our trip began. When I picked her up at the airport, I could already see we had a bit of an issue. The trip began because I had thousands of frequent flyer miles I could use for flights, but the airline stipulated that we must have the same itinerary. So, Nida had to fly into Chicago to board the plane with me. It was a minor obstacle—we were going to EUROPE! But there was an issue. Nida had a huge bag overstuffed with clothing. I didn't comment until we reached my apartment.

"The first thing we need to do . . ." I paused to make

The Well Traveled Guide

sure I had her full attention, "is go through your bag. I think you need to remove about half."

"What?" Nida was appalled.

"Well, I have this small luggage cart (yes, there was a time when wheeled luggage was uncommon), and your bag is probably too heavy. You'll see when we get inside."

I showed Nida the cart we would be using. It was a small wheeled cart that unfolded so you could stack bags for easy transport. The great thing about it was that it accommodated a variety of luggage. I had a job where I traveled every week for work, and it worked great. For the Europe trip, I had purchased a large duffel bag, and the plan was that we would stack our bags on the cart and roll away throughout the streets of Europe. Her bag was so big and so stuffed, I was afraid the cart would topple with the weight. What I thought was a large duffel bag for me became a small/medium bag next to Nida's.

"Let's see. Open the bag and we can decide what to pull out." I was being so practical! "And I've done the research. We can do laundry in Denmark when we stay with my cousin. We really only need clothes for a week at most."

Nida looked skeptical. "But don't we need things for the day and a change for evening? I can't wear the same clothes all day!" She had a point. "I've thought about this. We'll just take a couple of outfits for dinner. Since we'll be moving around from country to country, no one will know if we wear the same thing. And it won't get dirty since we'll only be wearing it for a few hours.

The Well Traveled Guide

Worst case, we wash a few things in the sink. Look, I have packed a little bottle of Woolite." Yes, I was so smug in my travel savvy, even though this was my first trip off the continent.

We started sorting through Nida's piles of clothing and began to whittle it down to the essentials. "For instance, do you really need twelve pairs of pajamas? I'll allow two." I continued sifting through. "Too many shoes." Nida began removing pieces. "You'll thank me later," I said. "This will make your bag so much lighter."

I think this is the hardest part of a trip—packing. You can't predict your activities, your mood, the weather, or even the local culture that will make you wish you'd packed that other sweater or the cute flats for the cobblestone streets. But this is what you learn as you go. It's also why so many packing lists exist. I seem to see a lot of "wraps" or "sarongs" listed. I never use either unless I'm in a country that demands them. And then I find it more fun to buy one representative of the local culture for a few dollars. It makes a great souvenir, and I can always donate it when I get home if I find it's not useful. Don't get too hung up on having the perfect outfit for every occasion. Your goal is to enjoy yourself and have fun—not be a fashion model (unless that is your profession, and then you probably have an entourage to carry everything for you).

Nida's luggage dilemma worked out to her benefit. While in Paris, her duffel bag broke! We ended up spending half a day finding a replacement. And she noted, thank goodness, that she could settle on a much smaller bag. It saved money and was even easier to manage! When we reminisce about that first trip to Europe, she laughs as she remembers how I made her repack her bag. A true application of "live and learn."

The Well Traveled Guide

Footbridge in the Himalayas, Nepal

The Well Traveled Guide

Chapter Eight

Gaucho, Patagonia, Chile

The Well Traveled Guide

How to Earn and Use Travel Points

Travel makes one modest, you see what a tiny place you occupy in the world.

—Gustave Flaubert

You've heard about travel points, you've seen the strategy mapped in movies such as *Up in the Air*, and you've even participated in trips courtesy of your diva points-obsessed friend. So how do you start to take advantage of travel points yourself?

How to Earn Points
Let's start with how to earn points. There are so many options for earning points these days that you don't even have to travel to earn points! You can earn them through credit card offers, online surveys, online shopping malls, dining rewards, and the classic earning venues of hotels and airlines. Some cards give extra points—often double or triple—for spending money on gas, restaurants, or telecommunications (like your mobile phone bill). Probably the most familiar and accessible are the programs the airlines and hotels offer.

Earning and Using Frequent Flyer Miles
Start early in your travel to collect airline points—register on your first flight. Even if you don't think you travel that much, you never know, and all the points add up. Pay attention to expiration policies. Some airlines, such as Delta, have no expiration date, while others usually require some type of point-earning activity (flights, buying miles, partner miles, shopping on their mall websites, or dining clubs) every 18–24 months to keep accounts active. Points are worth tracking. You can usually sign up online when you book a ticket, so make sure you start earning points the first time you spend money.

The Well Traveled Guide

Credit card offers are another regular enticement to gaining your loyalty and giving you miles in return. Review credit card offers, but be careful to understand the specifics and the obligations:
- What is the annual fee, and what are the spending requirements (such as spending $2,000 in the first three months) to earn the miles?
- How many miles will you earn? Is this the best offer?
- Look for cards that have no foreign transaction fees (since this is for travel!)
- You'll want a card that will deposit points into your airline or hotel account so the points can accumulate along with your regular mileage account (although there are also cash back cards)
- Evaluate other perks such as a free checked bag, double points for certain purchases such as at restaurants or gas stations, or ten percent miles back when you purchase an award ticket meaning you need fewer miles to purchase an award. Some credit card companies even offer travel or car rental insurance coverage.

TIP: Jump on offers extended when booking a flight or when on a flight as these offers might only be available for a limited time. I applied for a credit card offer with a $95 annual fee that earned me 40,000 miles after spending a designated amount in a three-month period. I used those miles to book a trip to San Francisco. While on that flight, they made another credit card offer for 60,000 miles, with a $95 annual fee, and the only spending requirement was the first purchase! I grabbed that offer and used the miles to fly to Europe for a summer trip. So, for $190, I had a free round-trip flight to San Francisco and another to Bucharest. I only had to pay the taxes. I probably saved at least $2000 for less than a $200 investment.

The Well Traveled Guide

The Points Guy (https://thepointsguy.com) is an expert on using travel points, and he has lots of advice on how to collect points. For instance, if I'm ordering something online, I'll use a shopping portal (United airlines has MileagePlus Shopping) to collect more points. Different retail stores may even have specials for extra points per dollar (especially around the holidays), so you can earn more points. Why not earn points when you already plan to spend money on something you need?

There are numerous websites that focus on travel hacking and how to best use the miles and points offered by credit card companies. Think about what is most important to you before you make your credit card selection. Even though you can cancel your credit card after a year, you won't be able to reapply to that credit card company again for a couple of years.

Hotel Point Programs

Hotels are also competing for your loyalty . . . and your dollars. When you book a room, determine whether they have a points program. If so, sign up online so you can earn points with your first stay. I started early in my points obsession and booked several vacations using free hotel rooms by remaining diligent in tracking my points. Programs change over time, and the number of points that used to earn a free week may only be worth a couple of nights now, but it still saves money. Hotels also offer credit cards that allow you to earn extra hotel points. One nice benefit is free upgrades as a card-carrying member.

The Well Traveled Guide

TIP: There's one drawback when it comes to hotel points: you can't earn points when you use services such as Booking.com or Expedia. They have access to lower rates, but is it worth the ding on points? You need to evaluate the price difference. It does take several stays to earn a free night, but you may have access to additional perks and services by leveraging your hotel status.

Additional Programs

Rental car companies often have partnerships with airline or hotel programs to earn additional points. And you can check the websites of your member programs to see what other ways they offer that allow you to collect points. As already mentioned, there are dining programs, shopping programs, and even partnerships with energy providers! Everyone is vying for your business by luring you with points. Research how many ways you can earn points on one transaction. Many hotels will also give airline points. Some of these perks disappear and reappear periodically, so it's important to check websites and ask when booking tickets or stays. Don't leave points on the table!

How to Keep Points

It always makes sense to track every program. I keep a spreadsheet that I check periodically to see if any of my points are close to expiration. Thankfully, most programs have the courtesy to email you a few months in advance if your points are in danger of expiring. But you need to take ownership of this, as some do not. For most airlines, you need to earn or spend points within a certain time period to keep your account active. It is easier now because there are even more ways to earn points. Even if I need to buy points or miles to keep an account active, it's worth it. I know people who plan

The Well Traveled Guide

short trips just to bump up and keep their airline status.

How to Spend Points
This is the best part of all! Airlines have a time frame for booking an advance ticket, generally less than one year in advance. According to The Points Guy website, it's usually about 330 days but varies depending on the airline. If you know you have a trip where you'd like to use points, do the research and find out how far in advance you can book. If you plan to use miles to fly to Europe in the summer, you will need to plan about nine months in advance, since the direct flights fill up fast. There are only a certain number of frequent flyer seats available. Some airlines will let you hold a reservation for a few days or a week before booking, which gives you time to check hotels, your friend's schedule, etc. before finalizing your decision. Whenever scheduling around holidays, know that everyone else has the same thought. Think about planning that trip a few weeks before or after key holidays to make the best use of your points.

As for hotels, review specials and book early. I will often hold a room at one hotel and keep checking other hotels that might offer better point deals, including the same hotel I'm already holding. Sometimes the point levels will drop, so I snag that deal and cancel the first reservation. With hotels, you don't even have to pay taxes, but sometimes I will charge a meal or drink at the restaurant or bar to give myself some points for the stay. It feels pretty good to check out with a zero balance or one under twenty dollars!

Ultimate Travel Hacking
Another travel hack is to use a credit card to buy a debit card, use the debit card to buy money orders for

yourself, then deposit the money orders into your own bank account. It creates a circle of money where you earn points but don't lose money, and potentially earn money too. The process is a bit complicated and relies on knowing where you can use the debit card to buy money orders, since many places won't do this or have dollar limits. In talking to people who are accomplished at this, they recommend buying $500 gift cards and using a credit card that gives several points for each dollar spent or will give you cash back. For instance, if a card offers 5 percent back on purchases, then spending $1,000 will earn you an extra $50. There are websites, such as Nomadic Matt's (https://www.nomadicmatt.com/travel-blogs/travel-hacking-101/) that give more direction on this. It takes time, but this can be a good way to earn points without any real outflow of cash.

Tale: If I Had a Point for Every . . .

I had a travel job when I was younger where my colleagues and I strategized points to no end. Major conversations took place as we challenged each other on how to double-dip to maximize points. In fact, our little group of travelers had so many points that it was a game to us—who could flash the most upper-level status cards and brag about the most exclusive free vacations. We joined every program and tracked our points by hand (yes—we lived an existence similar to wild dogs).

I had a shoebox tucked in my closet full of printed airline tickets, and when the statements would come each month, I was diligent about making sure I received credit for everything. Many friends were the beneficiaries, as I would use free tickets to bring companions on different trips. Where did we go? A free

The Well Traveled Guide

week at a Marriott in Barbados plus flight; a free week at a Hyatt in the Grand Caymans plus flight; two free flights to Europe; flights to California wine country for a long weekend; flights to Australia and New Zealand; two round-trip flights to Nepal; a flight to Vietnam; a flight to China; additional flights to Europe, Peru, Argentina, Ecuador, Africa (twice), and Maui (plus hotel); and a couple of trips to Saint Thomas (flights and hotel) and Mexico. The list goes on! I have used free nights sporadically for stays in Florida, New York City, Chicago, and San Francisco. Of course, it's much easier to track points through the airline and hotel websites now, and more people are collecting and using points than ever before. The moral of the story? Keep track and take advantage of the freebies!

The Well Traveled Guide

Chapter Nine

Tannery, Fez, Morocco

The Well Traveled Guide

Money

For the born traveler, travelling is a besetting vice. Like other vices, it is imperious, demanding its victim's time, money, energy and the sacrifice of comfort.

—Aldous Huxley

How much money do you need, and how do you access it while traveling? Planning for finances while traveling has become easier and easier. In most countries, you can walk up to an ATM and withdraw the currency you need. No more need for traveler's checks, no more carrying large stashes of cash, and very rarely do you need to find a place to exchange money.

As to how much money you need, that depends on where you are traveling and the experiences you want to enjoy. In many countries, such as those in Southeast Asia, you can book nice rooms and have great meals for a small price. As a rule, the more "westernized" the country, the more expensive it will be. Think about what is important—the experiences you have outside the hotel, or the amenities in your hotel? Since ATMs are the "go-to" these days, it doesn't hurt to make sure you have a couple of accounts and a way to link accounts if you run into problems. I'll admit that I use credit cards for many purchases—they are convenient, and I can add to my points stash. I advise you to track charges in case some nefarious person obtains your credit card number. Many banks send alerts for every purchase, so you'll know instantly if there is an issue.

Currency

Before you leave, check on currency and conversion rates. There are apps for your smartphone that make

The Well Traveled Guide

this much easier. You will also need to check on the availability of ATMs, which should be covered in a good guidebook. Some countries—such as Ecuador and Cambodia—will easily take U.S. currency, meaning you don't have to use local currency. Even my friends from the UK will often bring dollars, as they find it easier to change dollars instead of pounds. I usually carry $200 in U.S. currency. There is the perspective to not take more than you'd be comfortable losing. You need to think about what works for you once you understand how easy or difficult if may be to access additional funds in the country where you are traveling.

TIP: If you can get local currency prior to your trip, it can save time on arrival. Although most airports have ATMs in the arrival area, close to baggage claim, it can depend on the country. As tourism increases, it is easier to rely on arrival ATMs, but you still need to understand the exchange rate, so you have a good sense of how much money to withdraw. And pay attention to the fees—is it a percentage of the withdrawal or a flat rate? If a flat rate, then withdraw a larger amount to avoid additional fees later. The other option is the currency exchange windows, but the rates are usually not very good.

Be sure to take small bills ($5s and $1s), especially for Asian countries that accept U.S. dollars but never seem to be able to make change (Cambodia is one example). It will make life so much easier than standing and waiting for $3 worth of change while a street vendor runs around looking for singles. And it does not dilute your negotiating power when you only want to spend a couple of dollars but pull out a $5 bill.

For withdrawing currency, take two bank ATM cards

The Well Traveled Guide

(from two different bank accounts) so you have a backup and check for any fees the bank may impose for using the cards. Some banks do not charge fees to use other banks' ATMs, and I've found that many banks overseas do not charge a fee. With online banks, such as Capital One, you can open a second checking account, request an ATM card, and withdraw money at any bank in the world without a fee. You can also link the account to another bank for transferring funds if you run into an issue or find you need more money. It can also be a good way to control spending—deposit $2,000 and that's your budget for the trip. Contact your bank and credit card companies to make sure your ATM card will work overseas (it can be dependent on the pin number) and let your bank know you are traveling so they don't put a hold on the card for irregular activity. As banking evolves, offering security checks such as two-step verification, it may not even be necessary to alert your bank about your travel plans. Another way to prepare for a trip is to bring local currency with you. Some banks will overnight currency to you for a small fee. With my bank, I found the fee for euros to be about the same as the difference in the exchange rate, and it even included the FedEx fee. Super easy! It also eliminates the struggle to find a place to grab cash when you land.

TIP: No one wants to pay ATM fees. My strategy? I will try a bank ATM, and if it displays a fee, I cancel the transaction and move to another bank until I find one that does not charge a fee. Why pay the bank to get your own money? As travel dynamics continue to change, some banks now charge a flat percentage to withdraw money or charge a consistent flat fee for every withdrawal. It pays to understand the fees so you can plan best for withdrawals.

The Well Traveled Guide

TIP: For bank ATM withdrawals, always select that you want the exchange without currency conversion—that you want to withdraw in local currency. In addition, according to American Express, for credit card purchases, select local currency rather than having the transaction converted to your currency. These tactics should save you money on conversion fees. And make sure to check the three "Cs" before you leave the ATM: do I have my card, cash, and confirmation of the transaction (a receipt confirming the transaction is complete)?

Be careful when withdrawing money from an ATM as there are scams to take advantage of your status as a tourist. Make sure the ATM is at a legitimate bank. A walk down the street should be enough to see the major banks in a city, but country specific guidebooks will also reference key banks. Inspect the ATM and area around it just as you would at home to make sure there are no odd devices or cameras that seem out of place. I have found that many ATM vestibules in foreign countries have a security guard, which seems a bit more legitimate. I usually avoid the random ATM machines located in tourist areas as they seem to charge the highest fees.

TIP: Sometimes you can bring things to barter for souvenirs such as pencils, pens, or T-shirts. Steer away from candy or sugary gum for children, since dental hygiene is lacking in many countries.

Credit Cards
Credit cards make life easier and add to your points bank. Remember that chapter on points? Why wouldn't you use a credit card, especially for more expensive purchases like your hotel? Get a card that has no foreign transaction fees. I have a credit card that offers the

The Well Traveled Guide

added benefit of travel protection for any travel-related purchases on the card, such as airline tickets. I also accumulate points that can be used for future travel purchases. Is this the best card? That is a heavily debated topic on several travel hacking websites—everyone has a favorite, and the deals are constantly changing. More places accept MasterCard (isn't that one of their selling points?), but I carry a Visa card as well. American Express is . . . well, American, so not accepted everywhere, but the coverage is decent. When I was traveling for business outside the U.S., I used one without too many refusals.

Traveler's Checks

Traveler's checks are a relic of days gone "bye-bye." The only place I've been able to use traveler's checks in the last several years was in Tokyo. They were great for exchanging into local currency at my hotel, which was helpful, as it was difficult to find ATMs.

TIP: Foreign Tax Credits

When you purchase goods in some countries, they charge local taxes. Be sure to ask for the special tax receipt. When you arrive at the airport, you can reclaim the amount you paid in local tax since you are a foreigner. It can be a difficult process in some countries, but in others, such as Italy, it works very well. If you spend a good amount, it's money back in your pocket. I bought several pairs of shoes in Italy and received an instant credit on my credit cards at the foreign exemption desk at the airport. But you need to request the receipt when you make your purchase!

Cash—Carrying and Hiding Money

There is some debate over the best way to carry your

cash. A wallet in a back pocket seems like an invitation to a pickpocket, and in crowded touristy destinations, don't be surprised if your pockets suddenly feel lighter. Lots of people recommend a money belt. My feeling is that it can be handy, but do you want the extra bulk in your midsection? However, I do bring one and may only use it a couple of times during the trip. I like knowing I have the option, and since it packs flat, it's not an issue to include it. A hidden inside pocket with a zipper is another great option—many "traveler" type pants have the hidden pockets. But I also find that many designers omit these pockets for women.

The other thing I do is divide and hide my money across various bags, trying to only carry what I will need for the day. (That said, I try not to have too much cash on hand, since ATMs are almost everywhere.) I'm sure that most hotel service people are honest (because I like to think that about everyone in general), but leaving wads of money around is tempting. If there is a safe, you can use it to store your cash—although you need to be more creative than using 1-2-3-4 as your passcode. Some literature suggests that these safes can be easily cracked. I tend to think that creating any obstacle is often all that is needed to discourage theft. There are even devices that you can use to lock your bag that have built-in alarms.

Tale: No Money, No Ride

It was my first trip to India, and I landed around 2 a.m. The airport was chaos, even at that hour. I claimed my bag and then went to look for my prearranged ride. When arriving at odd hours, I usually arrange transportation. In this case, I was in India to do volunteer work, so the company had made

The Well Traveled Guide

arrangements for me. I had traveled with this group before, so I knew my ride would be there. I walked around looking for a sign card with my name on it as people scurried about, the heat oppressive even though it was the middle of the night. No sign of anyone to pick me up. I walked outside. Still no sign, but there were dozens of men milling about, attempting to hawk fares into Delhi. They swarmed me, hoping for a fare, and I kept refusing them saying, "I already have a ride." But where was my ride?

One man kept pestering me, and I told him I just needed to call my ride. I asked how much the pay phone would cost. "Ten rupees." Okay, I just needed ten rupees—but there was nowhere to change money at that hour. I didn't have a calling card either. That was all that stood between me and a phone call. Then the man offered his phone. I was skeptical. What did he want in return?

"One dollar," he said.

A dollar? Was he kidding me? That was closer to 100 rupees!

"What?! You know that's not ten rupees!"

He looked a bit angry that I knew that, but he backed off. I headed back inside the airport, wandering and wondering what to do next in my jet-lagged condition. A man holding a sign to collect a group saw me wandering about, encumbered with luggage, and asked me if I needed help.

"Yes—my ride's not here, and I have no change for the pay phone," I said, not even having to work at looking

The Well Traveled Guide

pathetic after a long flight, wet with sweat, and pulling a large bag.

"You can use my phone!" he said with a smile. I was wise to this scam. "How much?" He laughed. "It's okay. You can use it. No charge."

"Thank you so much. I have a ride arranged, but he's not here and the men outside were trying to charge me a dollar."

"No, no. That is not a good person. I will help. Here you go." He handed me his phone, I made my call, and within thirty minutes, my ride arrived, very apologetic as we sorted out the confusion. I'd had a schedule change, and the information never reached him. I felt just as bad for waking him in the middle of the night.

The lesson of this story is: know the exchange rate, and don't let anyone take advantage of you.

The Well Traveled Guide

Taj Mahal, Agra, India

The Well Traveled Guide

Chapter Ten

Young patients, volunteer dental clinic outside Hoi An, Vietnam

The Well Traveled Guide

Health

Once a year, go somewhere you have never been before.
—The 14th Dalai Lama

When you travel, staying healthy is important. No one wants to be sick when traveling. You've spent money to fly across the world, and an illness can compromise or eliminate your ability to enjoy your trip, meaning you miss seeing the sights and experiencing an exotic locale by becoming tethered to your hotel room. If you are planning to hike or bike or be active in any other way, you need to be healthy to have the stamina to keep going. And you may have to consider how to prepare for situations you wouldn't normally encounter on your home territory, such as evading malaria-carrying mosquitoes.

General Health

Be prepared by making sure you receive any relevant vaccinations (including the flu) a few weeks before you leave your country. If you take vitamins and other supplements, take them along, as you may be less likely to eat the regular healthy meals you have at home. Some people also take probiotics to eliminate stomach issues. In addition, it's good to bring an anti-inflammatory (such as ibuprofen) and acetaminophen (such as Tylenol). Remember to check possible interactions with any other medications you may be taking. Even over-the-counter medications can become a problem if you take too much or take combinations of the wrong agents.

If you are allergy prone, take your allergy medications, as you never know what sensitivities you might have at your destination. If you will be in a malarial zone, talk to your physician about the appropriate medication to take and make sure you understand the schedule since many require you to start dosing before you enter the malarial zone. The best defense is to avoid mosquito bites by covering up (which people seem to hate when it's hot), using DEET (at least 30 percent), and sleeping under mosquito nets. Check the net for holes, and if it seems to be a bit too well-ventilated, ask for a new one. I've had to insist on hotels providing one in my room when I've stayed in more remote areas. Sometimes they will list "mosquito nets" on their website but try to dismiss the need when I arrive. In some countries, malaria is so prevalent that they don't focus on avoiding it, but malaria can wreak havoc on your body and would be less fun than making a simple request.

Vaccinations
Most of us stopped thinking about vaccinations once we graduated from high school or college. Vaccines are for kids, right? Of course, COVID-19 changed that viewpoint to a great extent. Vaccines are also for travelers. Depending on where you decide to travel, you may have to treat yourself to several. Vaccinations are important, and I always make sure I'm up to date before I travel. It is much easier to prevent than to treat some nasty vaccine-preventable illnesses. Even a vaccination for hepatitis A will protect you at home and abroad from the occasional outbreaks. Some countries require or suggest certain vaccinations. Pay attention!

In the United States or other westernized countries, we enjoy vaccine access as part of public health efforts. The government has made it easy for children to have access to vaccines, and while the access is improving in most of the world (thanks to global nonprofits and health efforts), contagious diseases that are relatively nonexistent in wealthier countries are still present in developing

The Well Traveled Guide

countries or even reemerging in western countries. Recent measles outbreaks are an example. You don't have to do much research to discover that these diseases killed many people less than a hundred years ago. Be smart, be safe, and get vaccinated before you leave.

Check "Travelers Health" on the CDC website (https://wwwnc.cdc.gov/travel/) for specific vaccine information by country. It gives a breakdown of relevant health information by country and a description of the vaccinations you may need. And talk to your physician. I recommend finding an infectious disease/travel medicine clinic if available as they can help you decide what is most important for your trip. If you are traveling with an organized group, some companies will require certain vaccinations.

In general, you will probably need:
- Routine vaccinations (measles-mumps-rubella, diphtheria-tetanus-pertussis, chicken pox, polio, flu, and Covid)
- Vaccines recommended for certain countries and travel situations such as hepatitis A and/or typhoid
- Vaccines required for certain activities (if volunteering, for example) such as hepatitis B, Japanese encephalitis, meningitis, or yellow fever

The CDC website also has information on malaria or other diseases that need consideration and possible prophylactic medications.

TIP: Ask your physician for a vaccine tracker card. If you are seeing an infectious disease physician for certain vaccines, they will often have them available. It's a great way to keep track of your vaccines to determine when you are due for

The Well Traveled Guide

updates. For instance, typhoid is recommended for many countries, but the vaccine is only good for a few years. Before I plan a trip, I can easily check my card and see if I am due. It's also a good way to keep track of the vaccine type (sometimes there are multiple vaccine manufacturers for a disease).

TIP: Try to restrain from petting dogs and cats in other countries. It is so tempting, but strays could be aggressive, bite you, and transmit rabies. This also applies to monkeys as they can become quite feisty if there is food involved. Most people do not seek a preventive rabies vaccination, but if you are bitten by an animal that could be rabid, you will absolutely need post-exposure treatment. People who have been bitten by a rabid dog or cat in countries such as India or Morocco have died. Rabies is not a curable disease—if you don't receive treatment, it is almost always fatal.

First Aid

Below is a general list of first aid kit items that I've compiled over the years. Do you need to take everything? It depends on where you decide to travel. If you are visiting Western Europe, you can find most of these items at a pharmacy. In more remote or less developed countries, it makes sense to bring many of these items with you, as finding them can be difficult, especially with language barriers. I usually find that I am the one person who has the extra Band-Aid in my backpack or the ibuprofen someone inevitably needs and appreciates.

First Aid Kit:
- Waterproof tape and gauze

The Well Traveled Guide

- Ace bandage
- Band-Aids
- Moleskin (for blisters)
- Hydrocortisone cream (for insect bites or rashes from poisonous plants)
- Antibiotic cream
- Pepto Bismol
- Imodium
- Aspirin
- Cold medication
- Ibuprofen
- Acetaminophen
- Allergy medications
- Any prescribed medications (in their original bottle with Rx information)
- Vitamins/supplements
- Malarial medication
- Insect repellant
- Sunburn cream

Sleep

Many people have sleeping issues when they travel, but give yourself a couple of days to adjust before deciding on any type of sleep aid. I've never used sleeping pills, but I do use earplugs for the first couple of nights to help sleep. I'd rather be alert if I need to get up in the middle of the night for a hotel evacuation or other emergency, especially if traveling alone.

Try to adjust to the new schedule by staying up when you arrive until closer to your normal bedtime. The one exception I make is for traveling to Europe from the U.S. Since most flights arrive in the morning hours, I will check in to my hotel and, since the room is not usually ready, I walk around and find a place for lunch. By the time I eat and get back to the hotel, my room is ready,

The Well Traveled Guide

and I take a short nap for an hour or so. If you are light sensitive, it's a good idea to bring a sleep mask. Then I get coffee to push through until 9 or 10 p.m. when I finally go to bed. By the next morning, I am pretty much adjusted. Sunlight helps to reset your circadian rhythm, so it's always a good idea to get yourself out in the sunlight.

When I travel to Asia, I usually arrive much later in the day, so I push through dinner and try to stay up until 9 or 10 p.m. I also try to sleep for a few hours on the plane so at least I have a few hours of sleep in the bank for the first night. This process can also help with jet lag. I've read that you need one day for each hour of time difference. Not a comforting thought, when a trip to Asia means I need about 12–14 days to adjust. And then it's almost time to go home! I'll admit, it can feel a bit rough for the first few days, but I do adjust. I find that an afternoon coffee helps get me over that mid-afternoon slump.

Food

Depending on where you travel, your system may need to make some adjustments to your new diet. Try to mirror your home diet for less disruption, but be sure to sample the new cuisine! I think it's easier for Americans since we are exposed to so many different cuisines in our daily life. You can have yogurt heaped with fresh fruit for breakfast, burritos for lunch, and sushi with salad for dinner! You won't always find this variety in other countries—but then, one of my favorite things about going to Italy is having Italian food every day.

One of the most common warnings is to avoid fresh fruits and vegetables in countries where they may have been washed in tap water that would not be safe to

The Well Traveled Guide

drink. (See the section below on Water.) For instance, many Americans traveling to Mexico have made this mistake and suffered Montezuma's revenge, otherwise known as traveler's diarrhea. I think Montezuma traveled more than we know, because this affliction is not limited to Mexico.

The recommendation in countries with unsafe tap water is to only eat cooked fruits and vegetables. I have also found certain hotel or resort restaurants will use bottled, clean water to prepare foods, meaning you can have a fresh salad. However, you need to ask the restaurant whether this is the case. As tourists frequent more developing countries, it can be easier to find safe fruits and vegetables. As a rule, eat fruits you can peel, such as bananas. I've also used a hot water kettle in my room to boil water and then wash fruit with it (once the water has cooled!) with no ill effects. If you like milk, make sure it is pasteurized and if adding to your coffee or tea, you can ask for hot milk to make sure it is safe. The CDC website has additional information on safe food and drinks to give you a more complete understanding.

Food is one of my favorite parts of travel, and my palate has certainly expanded, so I find myself eating like a local. For example, I've learned that when in Thailand, I need to ask for "Thai" spicy. Spicy food evolved as a natural way to fight bacteria, which explains why hot places have hot food. If you think about it, it's remarkable how people figured this out in the age before refrigeration. For more information, refer to an article by James S. Thornton, "Why Do People Living in Hot Climates Like Their Food Spicy?" But I also know that some people can't handle spice or have other dietary considerations. Do some research on local cuisine before you leave so you will have some idea about available choices. It can make it easier to find a restaurant that will have some of your preferences, or you may be able to ask for certain food items. Finding food while traveling can be tricky for vegetarians, although vegetarian options seem to be increasing. Do your research before you leave your country! Remember that many cultures' cuisines are meat-based, so they don't understand the concept of being a vegetarian. If you bring some food items as backup, it will give you time to find appropriate options at your destination. Keep in mind that some countries will restrict what foods you can bring into the country, so be sure to check country government sites for more information. In general, I sample just about everything. When I start to have cravings for "home" food, I have always had success finding the ubiquitous pizza place.

Water

Can you drink the tap water? The U.S., Canada, South Korea, Japan, Singapore, a few countries in South America, and most countries in Western Europe have safe tap water. Much of the world does not. Check the CDC website for information on the water in the country you are planning to visit before you leave: select Travelers' Health, then select the country, and you will find a good overview of health information. Remember, if you can't drink the water, DO NOT USE THE TAP FOR BRUSHING YOUR TEETH OR WASHING FRUIT! The best way to approach tooth brushing is to pour some bottled water into a glass, dip your toothbrush to wet it, brush, and then swirl your toothbrush in the water to rinse. Using a small amount of bottled water is better than trying to rinse the toothbrush by pouring water over it (which I have seen people do). Don't be tempted to give it another rinse under the tap! I've also learned there are disposable

The Well Traveled Guide

travel toothbrushes you can use without water. I would probably reserve these for more extreme cases since they create more trash.

Drinking bottled water poses another problem—waste. Water bottles with filtration systems or water tablets can be safe options. I have used water treatment tablets for trips, and the trick is to have two bottles: one bottle "percolating," since it takes the tablets about thirty minutes to work, and another bottle ready to drink. This worked well for me on a couple of hikes through Nepal and in Peru, and I did not create unnecessary waste.

Altitude Sickness

Altitude sickness is not dependent on fitness level. I have been lucky in that I've never suffered from it, but I have friends who have been unlucky. If you plan to hike at high altitudes, many organized trips and even the guidebooks will recommend you arrive a day early to adjust. A good tour company will help the process by slowly ascending and building in extra days for your body to adjust. Drink lots of water to stay hydrated, and take it easy for the first day so your body can acclimate to the altitude.

Signs of altitude illness are usually dizziness, headache, trouble sleeping, and loss of appetite. And the only real cure is to descend. When hiking through the Himalayas, I saw strong, fit-looking men being transported down the mountains, riding on the backs of donkeys, the expression on their face betraying their altitude-sensitive condition. And since our bodies change with age, it can be a problem at different points in your life. There are some medications people take, but the safest route is to ascend slowly. If symptoms manifest and persist, you will need to descend. Another suggestion is to try a hike or

The Well Traveled Guide

trip at altitude in your home country before you try one overseas. You could consult directly with your physician on how to handle if you develop any issues. Altitude illness is serious. There is more information available on the CDC website.

Alcohol

Alcohol. The party beverage; the social barrier-breaker. You may think you know your tolerance, but be aware of what happens when you're already tired and jet lagged, dehydrated from the heat, hiking at altitude, and/or in a strange place. Remember to be careful of what you drink on the plane—it can be dehydrating. I always like to have a little wine on an overnight flight as it helps me to fall asleep, but I balance it with lots of water (not great for the person in the aisle seat who must accommodate my restroom visits).

If you decide to go out to a bar, never leave a drink unattended, and be careful what "local" alcohols you consume. You never know how you might react to something new, especially if you don't know the alcohol content. In general, if you are alone, or even with friends or family, remember that you are not at home, so stumbling back to your hotel after a night out could lead you into trouble.

Seasickness

If you decide on a cruise or plan to go out on a boat, ferry, or scuba diving, you may succumb to sea sickness. I have suffered from it one time, and I can tell you that I felt terrible. You know how they portray those poor people in movies? It's real. On almost every trip I go on, I seem to end up on a boat at one point or another, so it's good to be prepared if you know you are susceptible. A few years ago, Conde Nast Traveler published an article titled, "The NASA Space Treatment That Will Cure Your Seasickness," to give some insight into the condition and some suggested treatments. The author interviews a physician who recommends promethazine, a prescription-only agent, since it helps address the inner ear issues. And it's what NASA uses for space sickness. She does caution that it can be a bit sedating, which is probably better than the extreme nausea associated with seasickness. Again, it's about being prepared before you go, so your trip is not ruined by illness. If unsure as to how you might react, plan a boat outing close to home in similar conditions before you embark overseas. However, it may be a bit challenging to replicate conditions if you are planning to cross the Drake Passage.

Tale: Manta Chow

I had signed up for a day of snorkeling off the coast of Bali. We were going to Nusa Penida to see the giant manta rays! We set off that morning on a fast boat, traveling far out into the ocean to the small island. It was a rough ride, the boat bouncing hard against the water for over an hour. The boat had a few snorkelers, a few divers, and some dive masters in training. Almost everyone looked green, and I was shocked to see some of the more experienced divers throwing up over the side of the boat as we zoomed across the rocky waters. I was a certified diver and had been on many dives but had never seen anyone throwing up as we boated out to a dive! I had been talking to a Japanese woman who was going to be filming the dive, and she laughed about it, saying, "Yes, I used to get seasick, but not anymore."

And then the boat stopped. This was the spot. Everyone began to suit up and pull tanks for the dive. The boat

The Well Traveled Guide

was rocking furiously, and I began to feel a bit queasy. Once I jumped into the water, I'd be fine. Ah, the naiveté of the uninitiated!

I jumped in and focused on the guide, who was swimming toward the shore and yelling instructions. The waves were tossing me about, and I couldn't even see in front of me as I dipped into trough after trough, surrounded by the turbulent water. I'm a confident swimmer, but the tossing about was making it difficult to keep my head out of the water and make any progress.

And then it hit me. I had to spit my snorkel out as my breakfast erupted from my mouth. I could hardly hold my head up. What was wrong? This had never happened to me before.

I could see the guide looking about, trying to find his snorkelers. The three of us were hidden in the overwhelming waves. We made eye contact, and he shouted, "Here!" thrusting a ring buoy toward me. "Hold on to the ropes on the side." I grabbed the ropes, and the other snorkelers, faces drained of all color that denotes a live human, grabbed them as well. The ring buoy did help to steady me as the waves continued to throw us about. I felt so small, a tiny human in the big black ocean.

"I threw up," I said. The waves had quickly dispersed the chunks of my breakfast. Fish food, I thought. He nodded. "Yeah. It happens a lot out here because it's so rough." He was matter of fact. "But look down, the mantas are below us."

I shoved the snorkel back in my mouth, determined to

The Well Traveled Guide

push past the nausea. I dipped my face into the ocean, having learned on dives that if I could swim a little below the surface, the water was usually less violent. And then I saw the mantas. Dark shapes emerged from the deep, and I understood why anyone would endure this trip. The huge mantas flapped slowly past us, a ballet under the water, the dark beasts gliding about, unconcerned with the tiny humans around them. And we were tiny in comparison. They stretched a few meters from side to side, peaceful giants swimming among us. I broke back to the surface to try to steady the nausea that wouldn't leave, but it was hopeless, so I tilted my mask forward into the water and focused on the rays until the boat circled back to pick us up. It was no consolation that I was not alone in my misery.

Once everyone was back on the boat, we left for smoother waters. It was an amazing difference as we motored around the island, away from the wind and into the calm. My stomach remained unsettled, and the thought of lunch made me feel . . . less than eager to partake. But I knew it was going to be a long day and managed to force down some rice.

Eventually, we anchored in a peaceful cove on the other side of the island and jumped in for more snorkeling. Uneventful this time, denying the fish their chunky treats. The rest of the day was enjoyable for everyone as we motored to another spot later in the afternoon. It became a peaceful and relaxing day on the water, the nausea from the morning gone, the hot sun and cold water bringing me back to the moment I had boarded the boat that morning, anticipating a lovely day on the water along the island of Bali. Remembering the divers' reaction to the choppy waters, I pushed my last thoughts of embarrassment aside as we returned to shore to end our day.

The Well Traveled Guide

Chapter Eleven

Atlas Mountains, Morocco

The Well Traveled Guide

Technology

Travel and change of place impart new vigour to the mind.
—Seneca

There was a time, not too long ago, where you carried a phone card with you when you left the country. It looked like a credit card but enabled you to make long-distance phone calls when you traveled. That was about it for technology, except for a camera. Now, you could be carrying up to four or five items: a smartphone, a computer, an iPad/notebook, a camera, and all the cords, cables, flash drives, and data cards required to take, post, and store photos, watch movies, and send texts and emails. And don't forget your Kindle or other device for reading books.

TIP: For reading material on the road, you can download classics for free and/or check out books (including travel guides) from the library using Overdrive or a similar program. This works for phones and devices such as a Kindle, iPad, or computer. You only need a good Wi-Fi connection to download as you travel.

What is the bare minimum amount of technology you need? I think a smartphone is the bare minimum unless you are doing a substantial amount of writing and blog/website work as you go. With your smartphone, you can take photos, post social media updates, check email, read books, and even watch movies. But bringing along a tablet or laptop and an e-reader device will make for a more pleasant experience.

The Well Traveled Guide

TIP: If you are planning on relying on your smartphone, MAKE SURE IT IS UNLOCKED so you can purchase SIM cards in your country of travel, especially if you are traveling for an extended period. I try to find a phone-specific shop to purchase the card so I can return for help if there are any issues. The SIM card allows you to make local calls with a local number and access data as you do at home—very helpful when you are trying to find a restaurant or other sites and find yourself walking in circles.

To protect your devices from wear and tear, I recommend investing in travel cases. It's also a good way to keep charging cords with your devices rather than letting them snake together in a big pile like tangled necklaces. Don't forget that you will need adaptors for all your equipment; one adaptor should work for everything, but you may want to bring two if you anticipate having to charge multiple devices at one time. Another good tool is an external charging device/battery, so you have extra power if away from an outlet for an extended period. You don't want to run out of battery power on your phone if you are relying on it for photos and navigation!

For the most up-to-date information on all things electronic, check out Too Many Adapters (https://toomanyadapters.com). Founder Dave Dean and his crew review the latest tech and give complete overviews on everything you need to pack to stay connected while traveling. They also give great advice on country-specific SIM cards, purchasing and using mobile hotspots, the best travel apps, and Virtual Private Networks (VPNs). I subscribe to their newsletter for all the latest updates, as the tech world and the best travel gadgets evolve at lightning speed.

The Well Traveled Guide

TIP: When I'm traveling with a computer, I usually don't bring it out in public spaces. I tend to only use it in my hotel room. I might be a bit paranoid, but the less you advertise expensive equipment, the better. I also hide or lock my electronics in my luggage or safe when I'm gone from the room.

The following are some apps that I've found helpful in my travels:

GlobeConvert – It's helpful to have a convertor app for currency and measures, especially if you're from the U.S., since the rest of the world is metric.
WhatsApp – Probably the most used international app; you can use it to chat with friends wherever there's Wi-Fi, and it also allows for free phone calls.
Google Translate – Very helpful for quickly translating signs, but the app has also helped me avoid some "miscommunications" when there is a language barrier.
Google Maps or CityMaps2Go – This allows you to download offline maps so you don't drain your phone's battery while on the go.
what3words – An app to track your location anywhere in the world within a 3-meter radius. It can be used to share or list your location and can be used to find you in an emergency.

Tale: Lost in Translation?

I was in Bangkok, and it was hot. My friend Isabel and I had been walking in the heat for hours, investigating temples and other sites scattered about the city. Isabel was overheating and couldn't face walking another ten to fifteen blocks to get back to our hotel. So we decided to take a taxi. This can be an easy undertaking in many parts of Bangkok as many drivers do speak some

The Well Traveled Guide

English, but we were a bit off the tourist path. This driver did not speak English.

Thinking I was being resourceful, I pointed to the spot on my map where we wanted to go. It was a straight line a few miles down the road from where we stood. The driver nodded in agreement. Isn't it great when we can bridge that communication gap? We had only been driving for a few minutes when he took a turn to the left and started heading in a different direction—one that was not in alignment with my map.

"I wonder why he turned," I said to my friend. "Maybe he's avoiding a closed road?"

There had been protests that week, and some roads were closed. Yes, that must be it, we decided. But he never made another turn toward the direction we wanted to go. A more paranoid person might think he had some evil plan to take us to some secluded alcove. I took another look at him. No, he didn't fit the profile of "evil kidnapper." And how do you question your driver when you don't speak Thai?

When he finally pulled over to the curb and stopped, we looked around and realized we were nowhere near our destination. I think he also realized it when he saw the puzzled looks on our faces. I pulled out the map again and pointed to the spot we wanted, but he didn't seem to understand. Looking around, I saw there was a Skytrain sign halfway down the block.

I pointed to the sign. "Let's just get out and take the train back. We know there is a stop right by the hotel." Isabel agreed and we pulled out our money, expecting a

The Well Traveled Guide

fare of about a dollar. But when he pointed to the meter, we both saw it was many more baht than we expected, sending Isabel into a tailspin. "That's too much! He took us to the wrong place. I'm not paying!" she declared. "We can't not pay. We owe him something," I said.

We both sat for a second, deciding what to do as he waited patiently for payment.

"Wait, I have an idea," I said, grabbing my phone. Because I had a SIM card in my phone, I could use data, which meant I could use Google Translate! I wrote him a message to explain that we would pay a smaller amount since we had a miscommunication and now had to pay to take the train back. He nodded in agreement, and all was settled! International disaster averted.

When you travel, you can't expect everyone to speak your language, and you can't expect them to understand intended destinations when you point at locations on a map. I had something similar happen in Beijing where the driver resorted to driving me to an American chain hotel. It was not where I was staying, but an English-speaking woman at the front desk helped me sort out the right address with the driver. Many taxi drivers in large international cities speak a little English, especially if you are in a more touristy area, but be prepared to find a peaceful way to settle a misdirection of intentions. Remember—they are probably just as frustrated by the mistake as you.

The Well Traveled Guide

Chapter Twelve

Young girls on ferry in Myanmar, faces painted with thanaka

The Well Traveled Guide

Cultural Immersion

I dislike feeling at home when I am abroad.
—George Bernard Shaw

Culture is a tricky concept. It can include the food we eat, the songs we sing, the books we read, the movies we watch, the clothes we wear, the roles of men and women, and the ways religious beliefs influence our daily decisions. Certain cultural elements are very ingrained in some countries, so it is important to have some understanding of cultural norms before you arrive to avoid feeling like you've been stranded on another planet. Remember that you are a guest in the country, and you are expected to act with respect. If you don't like the culture or laws, it would make more sense to pick another destination rather than create a confrontation. An unfortunate example is how some countries handle same-sex relations. Ideally everyone would have the same opportunities to travel everywhere, but this is worth considering when you decide where to go: Is it worth being thrown in jail? As the world evolves, I hope all my friends will someday be able to visit any of the same places as me without any worries.

Some examples of cultural differences:
- In Myanmar, you make a kissing noise to get someone's attention.
- In England, refrain from using the words "fanny pack" to describe the waist pack or "bum belt" you have around your waist—"fanny" means something very different.
- In Italy, you need to cover your knees when entering a cathedral.
- In Thailand, there are strict dress codes to enter the Grand Palace: men must wear long pants,

The Well Traveled Guide

women must cover their knees, and no sleeveless shirts are allowed.
- In Germany, you indicate the number one with your thumb. If you try to indicate one with your forefinger, it is interpreted as two. The thumb is number one! (Remember the movie *Inglorious Bastards?*)
- Women must cover their head with a scarf when visiting a mosque.
- Littering carries heavy fines in many countries.
- Same-sex relations are against the law in many countries.
- Eating with the left hand is considered rude and unclean in some countries as the left hand is the "toilet" hand.
- In many Asian countries, patting or touching a child (or anyone) on the head is very offensive to Buddhists, who consider the head to be sacred. Showing the bottom of your feet is also considered offensive.

Another more complex example is a concept in China and other Asian countries known as "saving face." In essence, this is the gracious and compassionate act of saving another individual any embarrassment or humiliation when they make a mistake. This is something that many Americans or Western Europeans do not actively embrace, causing unnecessary confrontations and hard feelings. For instance, if your room reservation is flawed in some way when you arrive at your hotel or the taxi driver drops you at the wrong place, some people respond by raising their voice or making a point to bully someone into fixing the situation. That's not the kindest approach anywhere, but in Asia, it seems particularly offensive since their culture dictates another approach: you let someone know what

The Well Traveled Guide

they did right and hint at a correction rather than antagonize with a demoralizing verbal assault.

When in doubt, politely ask someone for advice. As much as I try to understand different cultures, when traveling for business it becomes a bit more difficult as the situation is more formal. I discretely ask someone I trust, always explaining that I do not want to offend anyone. And the reverse is also true. When one of my foreign colleagues made a faux pas that could cause an issue in the wrong company, I advised him of his misstep and provided some context. How else would someone know? He hadn't done anything wrong in his culture; it would only be wrong in certain company. Who would make the same mistake again if he knew? I found myself asking lots of questions when working in Asia and was grateful for the good advice people shared.

To me, understanding the differences in cultures is a constant "why" in my travels. Perhaps it is a general fascination with people and what drives them, but I tend to want to jump in and participate by eating the food, dancing the dance, and trying to "live" in another place. I often feel I can belong anywhere, a feeling of adaptability that not everyone shares.

Remember that you are a guest in any country you visit. No country needs to allow visitors, but I hope you think of it the way you would if you were visiting someone's home: be a gracious and considerate guest, adjusting to customs as long as no one is to come to harm. Besides, that is part of the fun of travel, learning about a new culture and understanding that although we may have different customs and practices, we are all human.

The Well Traveled Guide

Tale: Queuing in India

"Drink water. Drink water. Drink water."
It was our new mantra, and it was all I could do to continue forcing liquid between my resistant lips. My bladder had already advised my brain to keep my mouth shut. Not only did I feel like I needed to find a restroom every fifteen minutes, but since I was in the only place where you can get heatstroke in the sun and hypothermia in the shade, I was feeling the added effects of drinking continuous cold water on my body temperature. So now I was cold, and I had to pee.

We had arrived in Ladakh only a few hours earlier, and the guide was encouraging us to rest for the afternoon and drink plenty of water to help adjust to the altitude. I'm not sure how much rest we were getting since we all had to keep running to the restroom. But at that point in the day, we were too tired to do much else.

The journey began at 3 a.m. with a sleepy turn in my bed and the search for the lighted clock. The alarm continued to chirp at me, and I didn't want to be the one keeping the group waiting, so I climbed out of bed. It felt like an atrocity, and yet it didn't feel too crazy considering how late I was up two nights before, sitting at the airport, waiting for my ride. The struggle was not so bad, since it was warm in the room, and there was no temptation to crawl back into a warm space beneath the covers. And besides, the real adventure would start with this flight to Ladakh. That's why I was in India.

Soon I was up, I was dressed, and I went to meet the others in the lobby. Almost everyone else was there, the group of volunteers I would work with for the next week at a dental clinic in the Himalayas. A few were still

The Well Traveled Guide

slowly filtering in. Lalit, our local India guide, was hovering by the door, talking to someone at the hotel as he glanced over to the group. Within minutes, he walked outside, and we all gravitated to the door, pulling our bags behind us as we stepped into the hot dark night.

We rode to the airport, where our driver deposited us at the door. Based on my last forty-eight hours in India, it seemed like another typical stop in Delhi: people circling in cars, taxis, and buses and flowing into the building even at this odd hour in the morning, the sun not even showing its face. Flocks of people were crowding into lines that were so indistinct that what started as several lines would eventually merge into one and then separate again as each person or family aggressively crowded luggage and children into a new line. I had never seen such disorder in any country. Westerners know how to queue, perhaps an innate predilection and one that provides people with comfort. And maybe some semblance of order in an unpredictable world.

Our little army of volunteers leveraged our numbers by dispersing ourselves into a few different lines as we tried to figure out which line was real. We crowded and pushed to be competitive with our Indian friends. It seemed crazy. People were getting very angry and defensive of their positions, scowling and muttering unknown curses under their breath. We wouldn't know what they were saying; none of us spoke the local language, but we tried to hold our ground in the conquest for line superiority.

We finally worked our way up to the desk, trying to decide how we could divide up our numerous bags, since some contained supplies for the clinic, only to discover that we had just wasted forty-five minutes in the wrong line for the wrong airline. We were mystified. Our tickets proclaimed JetWay, but we were told that the actual flight was on Kingfly. So now we just had to find the right line, knowing we had less than one hour to check in. The advantage of having six of us was that we could send scouts throughout the airport in our second attempt to find the right line. In a matter of minutes, we had managed to locate the correct counter and drag our bags to the other end of the airport. We arrived just in time to find ourselves behind several individuals in a large group with only one agent to help everyone. We were all a little nervous—would we manage to check in and make our flight?

The woman leading the volunteer project wasn't with us because her flight had been canceled the day before. Since the flights were so overbooked, she was driving to the mountain clinic with a small group. The drive would take them a day and a half to reach Ladakh. We all discussed whether we would end up in the same situation. The flight was only an hour, but any fog in Delhi or Ladakh would delay our plans.

People were crowding the counter. The agent looked like a cornered animal as people yelled at him and waved tickets. He furiously typed into his computer, trying to find solutions. The crowd grew more and more restless. Women, men, and even children were pushing their way to the counter and fighting for his attention. He typed and typed but did not seem to find the right answers. John and Cynthia, two of the dentists for the clinic, stood with me off to one side watching him and watching the crowd. The environment began to feel quite hazardous with so much anger and pushing and the fact that so many flights were canceled with no backups. Lalit was shaking his head, looking worried.

The Well Traveled Guide

We asked, "Do you think we'll make the flight? Do you think they'll cancel?" I was looking for monitors or some other way to gauge our prospects. Suddenly the crowd seemed to gather energy and thrust forward again to the counter. The agent scrambled up until he was standing on the counter shouting, "Don't get PHYSICAL!! Don't get PHYSICAL!!"

John, Cynthia, and I turned away, shaking with laughter. I had visions of Olivia Newton-John in aerobics gear flashing through my head. I had heard stories about unpleasant travel situations in India, and I could not stop laughing. Even Lalit looked a bit surprised. Fortunately, the crowd seemed to become sensible again, and the tension dissipated quickly. The agent carefully climbed down and went back to his computer. We still had no idea of our own flight status, but the situation did benefit from a moment of unintended levity. And we made it to the counter to check in with plenty of time to spare. Flights were delayed for a few hours because of fog in Ladakh. In the end, we completed our journey that day.

Years later, when reading a book about the differences between various cultures, I learned that haphazard queuing was normal in India. And I'm using the word "queuing" very loosely. Apparently, it is common to have a group of people, in no particular order, confront a desk agent in any environment. Despite the chaotic-looking approach, it seems to work out the same—everyone eventually gets a turn. For the more conservative-minded Westerner, what appears to be a travesty of organization often yields the same results. It's true what they say, "When in Rome (or India)..."

The Well Traveled Guide

Chapter Thirteen

Terracotta Warriors, Xi'an, China

The Well Traveled Guide

Extended Travel

A man of ordinary talent will always be ordinary, whether he travels or not; but a man of superior talent will go to pieces if he remains forever in the same place.
—Wolfgang Amadeus Mozart

Lucky you, you've decided to take advantage of an opportunity to travel for longer than one or two weeks. One thing I've learned from my friends around the world is that vacations in the U.S. are rather short compared to many other countries. Their standard starting vacation/holiday is around four weeks versus a typical two weeks in the U.S. So, how do I define extended travel? I would say at least a month, in other words, the maximum time you can request a mail hold in the U.S.

Extended travel can differ from one person to another depending on the commitments in your life. It's more popular now for someone to work remotely for a few months from abroad or even pick a country and spend several weeks to better learn the culture and the language and live as a local. People think I'm adventurous for traveling around the world for five months and tell me, "I could never do that!" But the real questions are "Do you want to travel for weeks or months? Are you comfortable traveling with someone or on your own?" Extended travel is not for everyone, but it is an extraordinary experience that will teach compassion, resiliency, and the patience to look at a diverse world with new eyes.

In my case, I was the welcome recipient of a rather extensive downsizing at my company a few years ago. My department was eliminated, and my thoughts were

The Well Traveled Guide

not on what job I should find next but where I might go to satisfy my craving for something new. Winter was coming and the thought of exploring warmer climates was too enticing to pass up. Besides, I had been waiting to do an extended trip for years. And so I began to make my lists, lists that can help you plan your own adventure.

Extended travel requires more planning, more thought, and the ability to anticipate many things that are inconsequential when you are only gone for a few weeks. It is worth every minute of planning to feel like a real explorer as you move from country to country. For starters, what is the maximum amount of time you can be gone? Take full advantage of what you can tolerate or manage. I'm being realistic here. Some people are homebodies and may not want to be away for too long. But I can assure you—it will be an adventure you will never forget!

While more planning is involved, you don't want to overplan your trip. You don't want to compromise your ability to make changes as you go or limit opportunities to explore areas that weren't part of your original plan. However, you do need to think about country entrance visas as part of your overall plan. Can you obtain a "Visa on Arrival," or do you need to obtain one in advance? This will greatly affect where you visit and whether you need to plan "administrative" stops. Many visas are only good for a specific amount of time, so you will need to consider when to obtain the visa. For example, I wanted to visit Myanmar in February but was leaving the United States in early December. If I had obtained my visa prior to leaving the U.S., it would have expired before my February entry date. So, I needed to plan a stop in another country with a Myanmar embassy

The Well Traveled Guide

prior to entering Myanmar so I could secure a visa. I stopped in Thailand and arranged for my Myanmar visa at their embassy in Bangkok.

It's not too difficult to make all the necessary arrangements to take care of business at home before you leave, but you need to be organized. And you will probably discover a few things you didn't think about at first that will need attention before you board the plane. I've tried to provide a list that's as complete as possible, realizing that not everyone will need to complete all the steps. And once you've left, there are some safety behaviors you will want to practice on the road.

I've divided this chapter into three sections:
- Trip Planning
- Home Considerations
- Safety on the Road

Trip Planning
Let's begin with some of the questions and considerations that become important when deciding to leave for several weeks or months. Although you don't need to plan every aspect of your trip (that would leave no room for adventure), you'll want to consider some general motivations for your trip and what you want to accomplish or experience.

General topics to consider:
- Where in the world will you go? Deciding where to go and the order of travel can be dependent on your ability to obtain a visa to enter each country. If you have a general outline, investigate a Round-The-World (RTW) ticket at AirTreks (https://airtreks.com).
- Be advised that RTW tickets have restrictions

The Well Traveled Guide

(direction of travel, timing, cities that qualify, etc.). Depending on your plans, it may or may not be a good option, but it is worth investigating. I investigated a RTW ticket, but it was too restrictive for my purposes since I wanted to stop in some smaller cities and even some countries that were a bit out of scope.

- Will you be traveling with anyone? If not, can you meet any friends or family while traveling? Where could you meet? Or do you have friends or family in other countries that you could visit? It's nice to see a few familiar faces when traveling for a long time, but you will also meet people along the way. Test your comfort zone by going to places where you don't know anyone. I did an extended trip and built in some visits to friends I had previously made while traveling. I also coordinated to meet a couple of friends to travel together through Myanmar. It was a good balance to see people in between weeks of solo travel.

- Do you want to do any volunteer work in another country? Research the options, determine timing, and review how you can work the opportunity into your schedule. Most volunteer trips will cost you a few thousand dollars for a few weeks. The benefit is that you won't have to pay as much for airfare if you volunteer in a country you are already visiting or adjacent to a country you plan to visit. The experience is life changing and another great way to meet a new group of people. I did some volunteer work while on my extended travel, and one of the women connected me to her sister in the Middle East whom I later visited as part of my trip!

- Are you interested in sharing your experience through a website, Instagram, or blog? If so, think about what you want to communicate. Instagram is easy, blogs take a little more time, and a website is a more extensive commitment. I decided to create a website so I could add information as I traveled. At the time, Instagram was not so popular; most social media relied on Facebook posts, and I used that as my main communication tool.

- Set up social media accounts such as Instagram, Twitter, Snapchat, Facebook, etc. before you leave and let people know you plan to travel. It's a good way to share your experience and let family and friends know you are safe while traveling.
- Are there any possibilities to make money? This was something I considered with the development of my website. You could sell information, post Google Ads, or even link to other affiliate websites that sell travel-related services. It's why I eventually added affiliates. Affiliates are companies that pay you a small fee if someone buys something from them using a link on your website. For instance, you may want Booking.com to be an affiliate. If someone uses the link on your website to book a room, you will receive a small commission. If I stayed at a great place, I provided the name and link to Booking.com on my website in my travel summary. You may have already seen affiliate disclosures on other websites as it is quite common. It is a substantial time commitment, and you will need to decide what you are selling: Is it information (linking to a site with a recommendation), or providing a service such as booking and/or managing travel? Understand it will take you a considerable amount of time to develop and maintain a website, create content, and market your site. You

The Well Traveled Guide

can also pay someone to do it, but you'll need to account for the cost and manage the individual or service while you are traveling. Another possibility is to write about your experiences and eventually sell a book or articles specific to certain travel topics.

Actions to take before you board your first flight:
- Find a friend or family member to check on your house/apartment while you are gone or make arrangements for a house sitter. Make them a key and leave another copy with a second friend or relative as a backup.
- Determine what equipment you will need while you travel. Will any activities require special equipment that you need to purchase and test in advance? Also, consider the time to break in hiking boots, try a new backpack, learn how to assemble a tent, etc.
- Purchase travel insurance. You will need to purchase additional insurance, as anything offered through a credit card company won't cover emergency evacuations or general mishaps once you are traveling. I've used various companies over the years. For my extended trip I used World Nomads (https://www.worldnomads.com/row/) because they also offered rental car insurance. I've also used Insubuy (https://www.insubuy.com) to find a suitable plan. When I traveled to Cuba, very few U.S.-based companies offered insurance, and Insubuy provided the options I needed.
- Determine any medications you may need for the extended time and arrange to have several months of supply if you take any daily medications. You may need to contact your health insurance company and make a special request.

The Well Traveled Guide

- Plan a visit to your doctor to check which vaccinations or medications might be important such as emergency antibiotics and malaria medications, depending on the countries you plan to visit.
- Review finances and how to access money and accounts while traveling. You may need to link accounts and add someone at home to an account in case of emergencies. It's also a good idea to have a couple of different checking accounts with separate ATM cards so you always have a backup.
- Do you have a will? Have you designated power of attorney to anyone? These are documents to consider completing before you leave.
- Research the best credit cards with no foreign transaction fees and no ATM card fees; some even offer supplemental insurance and other benefits. Contact the credit card companies to notify them of your travel plans before you leave.
- Check on an international plan for your mobile phone and make sure to unlock your phone through your wireless carrier before you leave the country. Most newer phones are unlocked, so this may not be an issue. An unlocked phone allows you to buy SIM cards (a tiny card you insert in your phone specific to another mobile company/carrier) in other countries and use your phone as you would at home. When you are wandering through a city, you can easily pull up maps; look for restaurants, shops, or other services; and have a local number to make calls within the country. There are YouTube videos that will explain how to check your phone's status. Since this can change, it's best to check with your carrier/service provider. There are plans that now

The Well Traveled Guide

include calling and texting in other countries or even adding the service for a small fee.
- Set up relevant automatic payments for significant monthly bills such as your mortgage or rent. Make sure any payments that need to be made (such as those for utilities) are set up with an online bill-paying system or contact relevant parties to make payments while you are away. Although most companies have moved to some form of online payment, some still send notices through the mail, and you may need to have your house sitter review mail for you.
- Check to see if you can place your account on hold for internet/cable/phone service while you are gone. There is no sense in paying for a service you are not using. Some companies may charge a fee, usually much cheaper than paying for several months of unnecessary service or cancelling and restarting a service. I was able to put my home account (internet/cable/phone) on hold—a "vacation suspension"—for a one-time hold fee of $26.00. I also suspended my phone's wireless account for a three-month period, as the company only allowed a hold for three months at a time. Once the three months had passed, I placed another hold for the remainder of the time I was gone. The phone company even waived the normal suspend fee of $15. Tell your carrier to unlock your phone so you can use SIM cards as you travel. You can even find dual SIM devices in some countries that allow you to load two SIM cards and change networks when necessary. Use WhatsApp or another free text service (allowing voice calls and texts with any smart phone, in any country) to stay connected with friends and family and avoid extra charges.

The Well Traveled Guide

- Will you be gone during tax season? If so, you will need to file for an extension and pre-pay your anticipated tax before you leave. Send the payment via certified mail so you have a receipt that it was received. If other taxes are due, contact the taxing authority and arrange for your payment. In my case, my local school tax bill was due while I was away, and I contacted the local tax person to make sure I would receive the bill via email and could make a payment through my bank.
- Arrange a safe deposit box for any valuables (jewelry, documents, etc.) you leave at home in case of some disaster such as a fire; include a copy of your computer's hard drive in case your computer is damaged or stolen while you are traveling. Leave your nice jewelry at home. Flashing that fancy watch overseas can be a great temptation to nefarious types.
- Take photos of your home belongings and store all photos on your computer and in the cloud or Google Drive. If anything happens while you are gone, you will have this for insurance purposes.
- If you have hundreds of passwords, create a list for any you may need to access while traveling and create a password-protected document you can store on your computer or in the cloud. Or use a password management tool or service. You would not want to be locked out of your bank accounts because you forgot a password and couldn't reset it. This can be an issue when changing IP addresses as you progress around the world. The IP address somewhat "tags" your location when you log in from a device. When you travel and connect through a different Wi-Fi network, the IP address is different from your home IP, and some

The Well Traveled Guide

sites will flag this as a possible security issue. If you have two-factor authentication, you should have no problem accessing your site once you input a new code. Of course, if you have a different phone number via a SIM card, that can also cause a problem, although many authentications ask if you want the code to be sent through email or a text message. Just be aware that this can cause issues with email and other access to sites.
- Review all personal documents such as credit card receipts and make sure all documents are in order and easy to access if someone needs to pull information for you while you are gone.
- Review your airline and hotel points and their expiration dates since points can be a great asset on your trip.
- Check which credit cards offer insurance coverage for car rentals and call with any questions before you leave. Also, consider whether you might need an international driver's license in certain countries. My travel insurance covered car rentals in "Western" countries. Also, some countries will accept a driver's license from the U.S. Check the United States government website (https://www.usa.gov/international-drivers-license) for more information if you are from the U.S.
- Check your calendar to see if you have any appointments (such as doctor, dentist, etc.) scheduled while you are gone so you can reschedule in advance.
- Download a phone/address list to a document you can print. If something happens to your devices, it will be good to have a hard copy for emergencies. You may also want to load a copy in Google Drive or somewhere else you can access while traveling.

The Well Traveled Guide

- Download classics or other reading material to your Kindle or other device before you leave—you never know what Wi-Fi will be like in some countries. It's good to have extra reading material ready to go. Join the local library and see if they have a service to download books and movies (such as Overdrive, Libby, or Hoopla). You can check out eBooks (a great way to download travel guides too), audiobooks, or movies while traveling. This was one of my main sources of reading material as I traveled. For those who like audiobooks, you might consider a service such as Audible, which requires a membership fee.
- Secure your ride to the airport! Woo hoo! You'll be departing soon!

Equipment to purchase:
- Any necessary technology – computer, smartphone, tablet, etc.
- External hard drive or flash drive to back up important items; or arrange a cloud service.
- Luggage and packing accessories such as laundry mesh bags, packing cubes, compression bags, etc. You will want locks (in the U.S., you need TSA-approved locks) and may even want a cable that allows you to lock your bag to a stationary object in your room or elsewhere.
- Determine what kind of camera (and accessories) you want to bring. I opted for a digital camera with a built-in lens that allows me to zoom to 840 mm (a 35X optical zoom). I needed extra digital photo cards, a charger, and the connection/adaptor to download photos to my computer.
- Clothing – Do you need any special travel gear or shoes? Buy shoes/boots early and break them in; as to clothing, don't spend a lot of money. In fact,

check the local thrift stores; then you can throw out things as you travel if they become too worn or damaged. (See the chapter on Packing.)
- Snack foods – I would limit this as you don't want to have to carry extra food, and some countries are very restrictive on what you can bring in. At a minimum, bring snacks for the plane.

Home Considerations

If you own a home or even if you live in an apartment, you will need to prepare your space for your extended absence. This could include renting your space out or asking a friend or family member to move in and watch things or even take care of pets or plants. Another option is to have someone check in on your home on a regular basis. No matter what time of year, it's good to plan for some type of temperature control, as some electronics or wood furniture don't do well with temperature extremes.

Actions to take:
- Find your house sitter/pet sitter. Send an email with specific directions or information they may need while you are gone (see example below). Leave a printed copy at your house for reference. Ask them to walk through the house every few weeks to make sure there are no issues. They may also need to reset timers for lights if the power goes out. If you have a friend who is handy, ask him or her to be the secondary contact if your house sitter sees an issue they may be able to fix. I had a neighbor check the house but had another contractor friend as a backup who could help fix problems if they arose.
- Home appliances – What needs to be unplugged or turned off before you leave? I unplugged major

appliances that would not be used such as the washer and dryer. I also unplugged any lamps or other appliances around the house that would not be used while I was gone. It is best to turn off the water at the main valve. If you don't want to turn off the water, it is advisable to turn down the temperature on the water heater if no one will be using it.
- Appear to be at home. Use light timers or "smart" connections (Hue lighting, cameras, motion detector, etc.) to cycle lights on and off. Also advise close neighbors that you will be gone and give them an email to contact you if necessary. You may even want to alert the local police if you are especially concerned.
- Do any home appliances need maintenance before you leave? For instance, you might want to have the furnace or heating system checked so there are no issues while you are gone. In the winter, you'll want to keep the register on 55°–60°F to help protect your belongings from extreme cold. If you have regularly scheduled maintenance on other items, arrange for a different schedule. Some appliances, such as a water softener, should not need attention if you are not using water.
- Home services – Any services such as trash pickup should be put on hold.

Write an overview of necessary information for your house sitter:
- Contact Info—Leave your email, chat app handle (such as WhatsApp), and your phone number for your house sitter. Also make sure you have theirs as they may be able to help you solve international issues. Before I left, my cell phone provider assured me they had unlocked my phone. But

The Well Traveled Guide

when I purchased my first SIM card in New Zealand, it would not work because, apparently, they hadn't unlocked it. Big problem. On the provider's website, there was no way to contact them except by phone, which would have incurred international rates. I emailed my house sitter and asked if she could call the provider and get an email so I could correspond with someone. Once I had the email and could correspond with someone, I solved the issue within a day. Many phone companies no longer have customer service access via phone or email. They offer the rather weak method of inviting you to search a chat room for solutions. In my case, that did not work despite my most earnest attempts.

- Pets—Make all arrangements for your animals. I have "fostered" cats for friends at various times when they've needed a pet sitter for several weeks or months. I think this is the best option for any pet because they can settle into another home and have constant care. Even when I had a cat and would leave for two weeks, she was much happier on the occasions where I could leave her at a friend's place where she had company.
- Mail—Advise on when and if your friend will need to collect mail. I put my mail on hold every thirty days and let my neighbor know when the hold expired so she could take the bundled mail from my box and put in the house. Also, ask them to double-check that no packages are sitting outside the door or flyers are hanging from the front door. You may want to ask them to sort through your mail for anything that looks important and open it if appropriate. Some areas now allow for you to register for a daily mail scan (known as Informed Delivery by USPS: https://www.usps.com/manage/informed-delivery.htm)

The Well Traveled Guide

so you can track documents as they are delivered. It might be helpful in case you receive that wonderful call for jury duty.
- Plants—How often do they need watering? The best solution is to find an in-home plant sitter by relocating them to a friend's home. If you turn the heat down and have shades down, plants may find it difficult to survive for several months.
- Car—Is there someone who might like to have an extra car for a few months? It's a great way to keep the battery charged. Just make sure you and the driver have insurance in place to protect the driver and the car. Or if someone can drive the car every few weeks, that can also work. In my case, I was gone so long the battery died anyway, and I had to buy a new one when I returned. Leave the keys and access to the garage if needed. There are also trickle chargers you can buy for the battery when leaving a car for an extended time.
- Water—The best solution is to turn off the water at the main valve. If you don't want to do that, then have your friend walk through to check to make sure there are no water issues—turn on faucets, check for any leaks on pipes in the basement, and maybe flush the toilets so they don't get moldy. Consider turning off the hot water heater. If you decide not to turn off your water, then leave instructions on where to find the main water valve. While I was away, there was an ice storm, and the power was off in my house for a week. I had to make sure my neighbor turned off the water so the pipes wouldn't freeze and burst. It's a simple process, and it could save you from major headaches.
- Water softener—It should be fine since you won't

The Well Traveled Guide

be using any water, and you can fill it with salt before you leave. Leave an extra bag of salt just in case. If you turn off the main water valve, then you shouldn't need to worry about this.
- Heat—Let your house sitter know where to find the thermostats and which temperature setting you've selected, depending on the season. I was gone during the winter, and I set mine at 55°F. Change the batteries before you leave if you have programmable thermostats and leave extra batteries in case the batteries need to be replaced (usually indicated by a blinking light or a message of some sort on the device several days or a few weeks before they are dead). If the heat goes off in winter, then we are back to the frozen pipe issue if you don't choose to turn off your water.
- Light timers—Set timers on a few lamps throughout the house. Remember, if the power goes out, they may need to be reset.
- Doors and windows—Lock all your doors and windows.
- Plugs—Let the house sitter know if you plan to unplug everything in the house. It's a good way to make sure you are not drawing any unnecessary electricity while you are gone.

Safety on the Road

Most people are good people. I believe this applies all over the world. Think about it—how could any of us go about our daily lives if most people were not honest and good? But remember, there are people looking to take advantage of you, especially if they think they'll make some money. The typical scams exist, but I'm sometimes amazed at the kindness I've encountered. Approach people with kindness and they will usually do the same.

The Well Traveled Guide

Here are some safety tips to consider, especially if you're traveling alone:
- Don't walk down dark, deserted alleys at night (or even during the day).
- Go to ATMs during daylight hours on busy streets with enough activity that you are not alone; many have security guards.
- Lock your bag, even when left sitting in your room.
- Don't pull out expensive computers and other gear in public.
- Don't wear expensive jewelry.
- Divide your money. Only keep a few small bills in a pocket for easy access during the day rather than pulling out a large wad for small purchases.
- Don't leave a drink unattended in a bar or restaurant.
- Beware of strangers; if something feels unsafe, it probably is. In general, don't go anywhere with people you don't know. (I say this, but I have taken rides with kind strangers as many times as I've refused them.)
- Know how to contact the consulate for your country in case you need help.

Tale: Fiji "Uber"

I was staying at a small hotel along the beach in Fiji, and I thought it would be interesting to go explore the nearest town, more of a village in Western estimates, but a town just the same. Of course, the woman at the front desk would call me a taxi, but I wanted to go cheap and asked about the bus.

"The bus? Yes, there is a bus." She gave me a look that is usually reserved for a crazy person. "Are you sure?"

The Well Traveled Guide

"Sure. Why not? It's safe, right?" I threw in a smile, and she laughed. "Yes, it's very safe. You can catch it behind the hotel. Just go up those stairs." She pointed to the stairs at the back of the lobby. I asked about the fare and then thanked her as I headed for the stairs.

I looked down the road but saw no sign of the bus. It was hot, but rain clouds had already started to gather, a perfect day to go to town.

A car pulled up and a young man shouted at me, "Where you going?"

"To town. I'm waiting for the bus." His car was a faded relic from a previous decade. A woman was sitting in the back seat with a few bags and a young girl.

"Yes, I will take you."

Yeah, I was not going to jump in a car with a stranger. "That's okay. I'm sure the bus is coming." He smiled at me. "It's okay. I charge the same as the bus. I am already taking this lady." He looked harmless. And I could sit next to the door, one hand on the handle. Even the woman was smiling at me now.

"Okay," I said, nodding in agreement. He gestured at the door, I climbed inside, and away we went. A little further down the road, he stopped when he saw another woman waiting on the side of the road. After a quick exchange, she climbed in the front passenger seat. He drove the few miles into the town and dropped me at the bus terminal, careful to tell me which bus I could take back to the hotel.

When I returned to the hotel later, the woman at the

The Well Traveled Guide

front desk asked me about the bus. I explained that I had taken a ride on the way into town. She laughed and laughed. "Yes, that is what we do in Fiji. It is fine. But you?" She laughed. "Good for you!" And that was how I discovered the Fiji version of Uber. Before it was a thing.

The Well Traveled Guide

Chapter Fourteen

Spring in Tuscany, Italy

The Well Traveled Guide

Recommended Resources and References

Freedom lies in being bold.

—Robert Frost

We've covered a lot in this book. My sincerest hope in sharing this information is to motivate you to stretch beyond your normal boundaries and reach for the metaphorical stars. Your star may be in Italy or Argentina or Thailand, but remember, when you are looking up at the sky, we all see the same sun and moon and stars, even if the angle is different. And it probably means we feel the same warmth or awe at the wonders in this world when we take the time to look around.

For ease of tracking and perhaps printing, I've pulled together some references and checklists for you.

Travel Options
Below is a summary of travel companies and groups mentioned in the book.

Travel Companies:
G Adventures (https://www.gadventures.com)
Intrepid (https://www.intrepidtravel.com/us)
Explore (https://www.exploreworldwide.com)
REI (https://www.rei.com/adventures)
Exodus (https://www.exodustravels.com/us/)

Volunteer Travel Groups:
Global Dental Relief (https://www.globaldentalrelief.org)
Go Abroad (https://www.goabroad.com)
Cross Cultural Solutions (https://www.volunteerforever.com/program/cross-cultural-solutions/)
Together Women Rise (https://togetherwomenrise.org/learn/travel/)

The Well Traveled Guide

Electronic Resources and Apps
For the most up-to-date information on all things electronic: Too Many Adapters https://toomanyadapters.com

Helpful Apps:
GlobeConvert
WhatsApp
Google Translate
Google Maps or CityMaps2Go
what3words

Logistics – Transportation and Hotels
Train Travel: The Man in Seat Sixty-One (https://www.seat61.com/index.html)

Flights (many websites let you set alerts):
https://www.going.com/
https://www.kayak.com
https://www.expedia.com
https://www.momondo.com.au
https://www.google.com/flights
https://www.skyscanner.com
https://airtreks.com

Hotel Booking Sites:
https://www.booking.com
https://www.agoda.com
https://www.airbnb.com

Considerations when looking for a place to stay:
- Safety
- Distance from airport and main attractions
- Cancellation policies
- Photos of the venue
- Cleanliness ratings

The Well Traveled Guide

- Price
- Breakfast
- Amenities
- Overall reviews

Collecting Points: The Points Guy (https://thepointsguy.com) is an expert and offers advice on how to collect points.

Travel Hacking: Nomadic Matt
https://www.nomadicmatt.com/travel-blogs/travel-hacking-101

The Well Traveled Guide

Packing Checklists (from Chapter Seven)
You can also print the PDF provided on my website (www.wanderlynn.com). Look for Travel Tips and the page on Packing.

Clothing: If you have hanging clothes, put them in a long plastic bag (such as a dry cleaner bag) and fold over; it helps to keep them clean and wrinkle free.

Packed	**Item**
☐	Shoes—walking, sandal/flip flop, etc.
☐	2 slacks
☐	2 Capri type
☐	1-2 pair shorts
☐	Skirt or dress /Nice slacks for men
☐	Shirts—2-3 short sleeve
☐	Shirts—2-3 long sleeve
☐	Socks—4-5 pair
☐	Underwear—4-5 pair
☐	Pajamas—1 to 2 pair
☐	Fleece jacket
☐	Rain jacket (rain pants if hiking)
☐	Swimsuit
☐	Optional: Thermals for colder climates which double as pajamas

The Well Traveled Guide

☐	Optional: Scarf, hat, gloves for colder climates
☐	Optional: Hiking boots
☐	
☐	
☐	
☐	

Toiletries: Regulations for carry-on allow for 3.4 oz. (100 ml).

Packed	**Item**
☐	Sunscreen
☐	Toothpaste/toothbrush/floss
☐	Deodorant
☐	**Body lotion**
☐	Face creams/moisturizer
☐	Razor—you can protect the blade with a binder clip
☐	Shave cream
☐	Shampoo and conditioner
☐	Body powder
☐	Soap

The Well Traveled Guide

Packed	**Item**
☐	Lip balm
☐	Brush/comb
☐	Insect repellant
☐	Makeup and small mirror
☐	Tweezers, nail file, manicure scissors
☐	Small sewing kit
☐	Safety pins
☐	Small bottle of liquid detergent or detergent pods; detergent stick to remove stains
☐	Travel towel
☐	Q-tips, cotton balls
☐	Hand sanitizer (preferable to wipes which generate extra trash)
☐	Kleenex, toilet paper (in many countries, public restrooms do not have paper)
☐	First aid kit and medications* – See list below.
☐	
☐	
☐	
☐	

The Well Traveled Guide

*First Aid Kit

Packed	**Item**
☐	Waterproof tape and gauze
☐	Ace bandage
☐	Band-Aids
☐	Mole Skin—for blisters
☐	Hydrocortisone cream—to treat insect bites or rashes from poisonous plants
☐	Antibiotic cream such as Neosporin
☐	Pepto Bismol
☐	Imodium
☐	Aspirin
☐	Cold medication
☐	Ibuprofen
☐	Acetaminophen
☐	Allergy medications
☐	Any prescribed medications (in their original bottle with Rx information)
☐	Vitamins/supplements
☐	Malarial medication (if needed)
☐	Insect repellant

The Well Traveled Guide

☐ Sunburn cream

☐

☐

☐

Gear: Some items will be in your backpack for the plane.

Packed	**Item**
☐	Ear Plugs
☐	Camera, instruction book (or bookmark online), cables, charger, batteries, photo cards, etc.
☐	Cell phone, ear buds, charger, SIM cards
☐	Computer/notebook and case, charger, flash drives/external drive
☐	Kindle and charger
☐	Plug adapter
☐	Eye glasses
☐	Journal/notepad and pen
☐	Plastic envelopes for receipts/tickets/documents
☐	Headlamp/batteries
☐	External charger
☐	Water bottle/collapsible water bottle

The Well Traveled Guide

- [ ] Luggage locks/bag tags
- [ ] Guidebook (or load to Kindle)
- [ ] Small Swiss army knife and spoon—checked bags only!
- [ ] Duct tape—wrap a decent amount around a pencil; an amazing "fix it" tool
- [ ] Hydration tablets
- [ ] Portable laundry line
- [ ] Money belt
- [ ] Extra duffel/bag for carry-on souvenirs
- [ ] **Trekking poles—if hiking**
- [ ] Sleeping bag liner—provides extra warmth and a safe cocoon for questionable bed linens
- [ ] Zip lock bags—multiple uses and reuses
- [ ] Sunglasses with UV protection
- [ ] Sink stopper/plug for doing laundry in the sink
- [ ] Small travel umbrella—can also be used for the sun
- [ ] Optional: Mask/snorkel
- [ ]
- [ ]
- [ ]

The Well Traveled Guide

For the Plane:

Packed	Item
☐	Passport and copy (pack copy in a separate bag)
☐	Visas for the country you are visiting, if needed
☐	Credit cards/ATM cards
☐	Vaccination card (if applicable)
☐	Driver's license for car rentals
☐	Plane tickets or boarding passes (if not electronic)
☐	Cash
☐	Travel insurance documents
☐	Neck pillow
☐	Change of clothes if you are checking a bag
☐	Snacks/gum
☐	Reading material/Books/Kindle
☐	Computer/Smart Phone/Tablet
☐	Camera
☐	
☐	
☐	

The Well Traveled Guide

Extended Leave Preparation Checklists (from Chapter Thirteen)

You can also print the PDF provided on my website (www.wanderlynn.com). Look for Travel Tips and the page on Planning Your Trip.

Actions to take before boarding your first flight:

Complete	Task
☐	Find a friend or family member to check on your house/apartment
☐	Determine what equipment you will need as you travel
☐	Purchase travel insurance
☐	Determine any medications you may need to bring
☐	Plan a visit to your doctor to check on necessary vaccinations or medications
☐	Review finances and access to money and accounts while traveling
☐	Complete will and designated power of attorney
☐	Research the best credit cards
☐	Check on an international plan for your mobile phone and *make SURE* to unlock your phone through your wireless carrier
☐	Set up relevant auto-payments for significant monthly bills
☐	Put internet/cable/phone service accounts on hold as necessary
☐	Set up WhatsApp or another free text service to communicate with friends/family

The Well Traveled Guide

Complete	Task
☐	Taxes—pay in advance if relevant
☐	Arrange a safe deposit box for any valuables
☐	Take photos of your home belongings and store all photos on your computer and in the cloud or Google Drive, etc.
☐	If you have hundreds of passwords, create a secure list for access while traveling
☐	Review all personal documents that may be important while you are traveling
☐	Review your airline and hotel points and expirations
☐	Check which credit cards offer insurance coverage for car rentals and call with any questions before you leave
☐	Check the need for an international driver's license
☐	Check your calendar to see if you have any appointments to reschedule
☐	Create and print a phone/address list
☐	Download free classics or other reading material to your Kindle
☐	Review home appliances and systems that may need servicing or monitoring
☐	Appear to be "at home" by using light timers or "smart" connections
☐	Home services, such as the trash, should be put on hold

The Well Traveled Guide

☐ Secure your ride to the airport
☐
☐
☐

Write an overview of necessary information for your house sitter concerning:

Complete   **Task**

☐ Provide your contact info (email, WhatsApp, phone number, etc.)

☐ Pets—what care may be needed

☐ Mail handling

☐ Plant care

☐ Car care or maintenance needed

☐ Water—how to turn off if necessary

☐ Any appliances needing attention

☐ Heating or cooling settings

☐ Timer lights

☐ Alarm System/Doors and windows

☐ Plugs—what should be plugged in and what is not (specific lamps and appliances)

The Well Traveled Guide

☐
☐
☐

Equipment to purchase:

Complete   **Task**

☐ Any necessary technology including an external hard drive or flash drive to back up important information and/or arrange a cloud service

☐ Luggage and packing accessories including locks

☐ Camera (and accessories)

☐ Food/snacks

☐ Any necessary clothing

☐
☐
☐

The Well Traveled Guide

Endnotes

For travel information on places I have visited, check my website, www.wanderlynn.com. I share useful information for fellow travelers.

Good travel guides have supported my adventures throughout the years including *Lonely Planet, Frommer's, The Real Guide, Fodor's, National Geographic Traveler, Rick Steves', Moon Travel Handbooks, Time Out,* and *Rough Guides*. Many of these books are further complemented by websites offering information. Never assume you know everything. I constantly check other sources and subscribe to travel focused newsletters to stay informed and current.

A Journey of One's Own by Thalia Zepatos was inspiration and a foundation for my first solo international trip many years ago.

Additional website references:
Google Alerts—
https://support.google.com/websearch/answer/4815696?hl=en

U.S. Department of State—passports, visas, country specific travel information; https://www.state.gov/travelers/

Trusted Traveler website—TSA PreCheck and Global Entry; https://www.dhs.gov/trusted-traveler-programs

CIBT—passport and visa services; https://cibtvisas.com

European Union visas—https://travel-europe.europa.eu/etias_en

The Well Traveled Guide

Country Exit Visa Information—https://www.tripzilla.com/countries-departure-tax/77780

Travelers' rights (EU)—(EC) No 261/2004 – https://eur-lex.europa.eu/legal-content/EN/TXT/HTML/?uri=CELEX%3A32004R0261

Travelers' rights (USA)—U.S. Department of Transportation – https://www.transportation.gov/

World Nomads Travel Insurance—https://www.worldnomads.com/row/

Insubuy Travel Insurance—https://www.insubuy.com

American Express recommendation on ATM and credit card currency—https://www.americanexpress.com/en-us/credit-cards/credit-intel/should-you-pay-in-local-or-home-currency-when-traveling/

International Driver's License—https://www.usa.gov/international-drivers-license

Centers for Disease Control and Prevention (information on travelers' health)—https://wwwnc.cdc.gov/travel/

Food—Why Do People Living in Hot Climates Like Their food Spicy? By James S. Thorton; https://www.ncbi.nlm.nih.gov/pmc/articles/PMC4861189/

Seasickness—The NASA Space Treatment That Will Cure Your Seasickness; Conde Nast Traveler
https://www.cntraveler.com/stories/2016-07-21/the-nasa-space-treatment-that-will-cure-your-seasickness

The Well Traveled Guide

Overdrive (requires a library subscription/membership)—https://www.overdrive.com

Libby (requires a library subscription/membership)—https://www.overdrive.com/apps/libby

Hoopla (requires a library subscription/membership)—https://www.hoopladigital.com

Audible—https://www.audible.com

The Well Traveled Guide

Acknowledgements

There are many people to thank, some who were fellow travelers along the way whose names I've never known or have forgotten, who offered tips and advice that became part of my approach to travel. Sharing of stories and information is one of the key parts of making travel fun and accessible to everyone.

And then there are my friends who listened to my ideas for this book and did a pre-read or offered input to let me know what worked and what needed revision: Anne Yirak, Elizabeth Venart, Joyce Ercolino, Kari Gearhart, Lauren O'Brien, Linda Knight, Mike Petro, Robin Bender Stevens, Sally Silverman, Susan Yirak, and Terry Leahy. Thanks to Maryfrances Wagner, who encouraged my writing from an early age; my copy editor, Jessica Filippi; my proofreader Pat Lawson; cover designer Domingo Morales; and book designer Greg Field. Everyone's help and support was invaluable in helping me complete this book.

And a final thank you to everyone for helping me to reach anyone with a dream to travel more and travel wise!

The Well Traveled Guide

About the Author

Lynn Doerr is an author, consultant, and a curious traveler and explorer. Her passion for exploration is fueled by early days paging through *National Geographic* magazines, while plotting her intentions to travel far and wide. Lynn has visited over sixty countries and territories, collecting and sharing travel information with friends and family. Her goal is not to tick countries off a list but to set both feet in a country and spend time wandering, with an emphasis on time spent outdoors and to attempt, in a conscious way, to better understand this planet. And, of course, to meet the delightful and special people who populate our earth.

Volunteering at dental clinic in Cambodia (fourth from the left).

Lynn has a degree in journalism from the University of Missouri and a master's in marketing communications from Northwestern. When not on distant shores, Lynn is a consultant in marketing and market research and also writes for local publications. In her free time, Lynn volunteers in her local community by serving on multiple

The Well Traveled Guide

boards. She also enjoys enjoys horseback riding, running, hiking, and mountain biking through local preserves, always curious as to where the next trail will lead. She lives in the suburbs of Philadelphia.

For more information, please check her website dedicated to more travel wisdom and tips:
www.wanderlynn.com

The Well Traveled Guide

www.ingramcontent.com/pod-product-compliance
Lightning Source LLC
Chambersburg PA
CBHW070807230426
43665CB00017B/2521